D1559329

THE 1990 DEFENSE BUDGET

Studies in Defense Policy

THE 1990 DEFENSE BUDGET

William W. Kaufmann and
Lawrence J. Korb

THE BROOKINGS INSTITUTION
Washington, D.C.

THE BROOKINGS INSTITUTION

The Brookings Institution is an independent organization devoted to nonpartisan research, education, and publication in economics, government, foreign policy, and the social sciences generally. Its principal purposes are to aid in the development of sound public policies and to promote public understanding of issues of national importance.

The Institution was founded on December 8, 1927, to merge the activities of the Institute for Government Research, founded in 1916, the Institute of Economics, founded in 1922, and the Robert Brookings Graduate School of Economics and Government, founded in 1924.

The Board of Trustees is responsible for the general administration of the Institution, while the immediate direction of the policies, program, and staff is vested in the President, assisted by an advisory committee of the officers and staff. The by-laws of the Institution state: "It is the function of the Trustees to make possible the conduct of scientific research, and publication, under the most favorable conditions, and to safeguard the independence of the research staff in the pursuit of their studies and in the publication of the results of such studies. It is not a part of their function to determine, control, or influence the conduct of particular investigations or the conclusions reached."

The President bears final responsibility for the decision to publish a manuscript as a Brookings book. In reaching his judgment on the competence, accuracy, and objectivity of each study, the President is advised by the director of the appropriate research program and weighs the views of a panel of expert outside readers who report to him in confidence on the quality of the work. Publication of a work signifies that it is deemed a competent treatment worthy of public consideration but does not imply endorsement of conclusions or recommendations.

The Institution maintains its position of neutrality on issues of public policy in order to safeguard the intellectual freedom of the staff. Hence interpretations or conclusions in Brookings publications should be understood to be solely those of the authors and should not be attributed to the Institution, to its trustees, officers, or other staff members, or to the organizations that support its research.

FOREWORD

On February 9, 1989, President Bush froze defense spending for fiscal year 1990 at the 1989 level and proposed only small inflation-adjusted increases for the next three years. His announcement obviously signals an end to the unprecedented peacetime expansion of defense programs and budgets of the Reagan administration. But freezing the budget does not resolve the disparity between the projected costs of existing force structure and programs and the limited funding that will now be available, a disparity that may easily exceed $200 billion by 1994.

In this study of the defense budget for 1990 and beyond, William W. Kaufmann and Lawrence J. Korb review the military buildup and five-year defense plans of the second Reagan term. Then, considering likely international situations and U.S. military requirements and commitments, the authors present flexible, pragmatic, and detailed proposals that would allow America's conventional and nuclear forces to maintain preparedness within a budget more limited than any envisioned just a few years ago.

William W. Kaufmann is a consultant to the Foreign Policy Studies program of the Brookings Institution and a lecturer at the John F. Kennedy School of Government at Harvard University. Lawrence J. Korb, a former assistant secretary of defense, is the director of Brookings' Center for Public Policy Education and a senior fellow.

The authors wish to thank John D. Steinbruner for his comments; James R. Schneider for editing the manuscript; Ethan Gutmann, Vernon L. Kelly, and Andrew Scobell for verifying the sources; and Ann M. Ziegler, Marlene C. Perfitte, and Susan L. Woolen for preparing the manuscript for publication.

Brookings gratefully acknowledges financial support for this study by the John D. and Catherine T. MacArthur Foundation and the Carnegie Corporation of New York.

The views expressed in this study are those of the authors and should not be ascribed to trustees, officers, or other staff members of the Brookings Institution.

BRUCE K. MAC LAURY
President

April 1989
Washington, D.C.

THE 1990 DEFENSE BUDGET

THE 1990 DEFENSE BUDGET

GEORGE SANTAYANA once observed that the "working of great institutions is mainly the result of a vast mass of routine, petty malice, self interest, carelessness, and sheer mistake. Only a residual fraction is thought." Whether or not they were aware of this gloomy pronouncement, presidents from Eisenhower to Carter believed that at the outset of their administrations they should demand some systematic analysis from the Department of Defense about its goals, programs, and budgets. President Bush has wisely decided that his administration too should undertake a review.

Such a comprehensive review is badly needed: as W. Somerset Maugham once noted, the "unfortunate thing about this world is that good habits are so much easier to give up than bad ones." Since 1977 no group within the Defense Department has seriously and systematically examined the assumptions either of its political predecessors or of its own policymakers.[1] As a consequence, President Bush faces not only a complex and disturbing legacy from the Reagan administration but also a number of difficult decisions. Indeed, it is impossible to separate the nature of his choices

---

1. Ironically, in the last year of the Reagan administration, the secretary of defense and the assistant to the president for national security affairs established a commission on integrated long-term strategy. Cochaired by the undersecretary of defense for policy, Fred C. Iklé, and by Albert Wohlstetter, the commission produced *Discriminate Deterrence*, a report that attempted to relate programs to future budgets. The study urged the department to deemphasize forces that would be used primarily in a large-scale conventional war in Europe or an all-out nuclear exchange. Instead Iklé and Wohlstetter assigned budgetary priority to those forces that could be employed in low-intensity conflict and limited nuclear contingencies. Within this focus, the study argued that precision guidance weapons munitions (smart weapons) should take priority over new weapons platforms and that weapons modernization be pursued at the expense of readiness. Finally, the report noted the growing importance of the Pacific rim as an area of strategic importance to the United States. Even more ironically, Iklé resigned shortly after completing the report and no action was taken on it. See Commission on Integrated Long-Term Strategy, *Discriminate Deterrence* (January 1988).

from an appreciation of the Reagan legacy and the context in which these choices must now be made.

The Reagan Legacy

Harold Macmillan, former prime minister of the United Kingdom, has commented, ''I have never found in a long experience of politics that criticism is ever inhibited by ignorance.'' Certainly as he entered office in 1981 Ronald Reagan brought with him misconceptions that had formed an integral part of the Republican platform in 1980. He was convinced that he was inheriting a decade of neglect in defense, even though budget authority for fiscal 1981 was already greater than it had been in fiscal 1964, the last pre-Vietnam budget year.[2] Indeed, despite inflation, defense budget authority had increased in real terms in fiscal 1980 and 1981. In addition, presidents Nixon, Ford, and Carter had already inaugurated substantial programs for modernizing nuclear and conventional forces.[3]

Reagan expressed special concern about what was known as the window of vulnerability—a vulnerability based on the supposition that U.S. intercontinental ballistic missiles were the heart of the strategic nuclear deterrent and could be destroyed in a Soviet first strike—despite analyses showing that even after a first strike, residual U.S. forces should be able to deliver more than 3,000 warheads to a wide range of targets in the Soviet Union.[4] Reagan and his key advisers had also been persuaded on quite tenuous grounds that the United States was losing its naval superiority to the Soviet Union and could restore it only by building a 600-ship fleet dominated by 15 carrier battle groups, 4 surface action groups with battleships at their center, 100 modern nuclear attack submarines, and an expanded amphibious assault force.[5]

In addition, Reagan held two other views that were to influence strongly his defense legacy. He and his advisers were convinced that the Soviet Union was outspending the United States in defense by as much as 50 percent and that the Soviet advantage in investment in new weapons was

2. Office of the Assistant Secretary of Defense (Comptroller), *National Defense Budget Estimates for FY 1988–1989* (May 1987), table 6-9.

3. Melvin R. Laird, ''A Strong Start in a Difficult Decade: Defense Policy in the Nixon-Ford Years,'' *International Security*, vol. 10 (Fall 1985), pp. 5–26.

4. William W. Kaufmann, *A Reasonable Defense* (Brookings, 1986), table 5-9.

5. *Department of Defense Annual Report, Fiscal Year 1983*, pp. II-14–II-15, III-19–III-36.

even greater. They also believed, as had (briefly) others before them, that many of these weaknesses had come from centralized planning and programming decisions in the Office of the Secretary of Defense and that the remedy was to limit the powers of OSD and give greater latitude to the Army, the Navy, the Marine Corps, and the Air Force within what would be generous budgets.[6]

Fiscal 1981–85

Based on these somewhat sketchy views of what needed to be done to restore U.S. defenses, President Reagan, with considerable support from Congress, began an unprecedented peacetime expansion of the defense budget. Overall budget authority for defense increased from fiscal 1980 to 1985 in real terms by nearly 53 percent (table 1). More remarkably, investment (which includes procurement, research, development, testing, and evaluation and military construction) grew in real terms by more than 100 percent, and procurement alone by 112 percent. This meant that during these five years U.S. budget authority was expanding at a real rate of more than 10 percent a year and defense outlays (as differentiated from budget authority) by more than 6 percent a year, while Soviet spending was increasing by no more than 2 percent a year (as estimated by the Central Intelligence Agency), and its investment outlays were not growing in real terms at all.[7]

Several other features of these Reagan budgets are worth noting. The budgets were front-end loaded in favor of investment, especially procurement. This meant that because of the long lead times associated with the expansion of production lines and the actual production of missiles, aircraft, ships, and tracked vehicles, the growth in spending would lag behind the growth in budget authority (which allows a department to sign contracts and ensures that the necessary funds will be available when bills come due). It also meant that other important accounts, such as military personnel and operation and maintenance, would not have to increase at comparable rates until some years in the future. As it was, the budget for

---

6. *Department of Defense Annual Report, Fiscal Year 1983,* pp. II-4–II-6; and Vincent Puritano and Lawrence Korb, "Streamlining PPBS to Better Manage National Defense," *Public Administration Review,* vol. 41 (September-October 1981), pp. 569–74. The Republican platform of 1980 went so far as to call for the abolition of the Office of Systems Analysis.

7. William W. Kaufmann, "A Defense Agenda for Fiscal Years 1990–1994," in John D. Steinbruner, ed., *Restructuring American Foreign Policy* (Brookings, 1989), p. 57.

Table 1. Department of Defense Budget Authority, by Appropriation Title, Fiscal Years 1980–85

Billions of fiscal 1988 dollars unless otherwise specified

Title	1980	1981	1982	1983	1984	1985	Percent real change 1980–85
Authority							
Military personnel	68.1	69.8	71.8	73.4	74.9	75.3	10.6
Operation and maintenance	62.6	68.0	72.3	75.5	79.4	84.4	34.8
Procurement	50.3	63.1	79.5	94.5	97.9	106.7	111.9
Research, development, test, and evaluation	19.1	21.5	24.6	26.9	30.6	34.5	81.0
Military construction	3.1	4.4	6.0	5.3	5.2	6.1	95.5
Family housing	2.1	2.5	2.6	3.1	3.0	3.2	51.4
Other[a]	0.9	2.7	2.2	0.8	2.4	5.1	b
Total	206.2	232.0	259.0	279.5	293.4	315.3	52.9
Outlays	199.8	209.0	224.0	240.9	250.7	269.3	34.7

Source: Office of the Assistant Secretary of Defense (Comptroller), *National Defense Budget Estimates for FY 1988/1989*, pp. 94, 103.

a. Special foreign currency program, revolving and management funds, and trust funds, receipts, and accruals.

b. Year-to-year variations make percentage change meaningless.

military personnel, on the average, grew in real terms by only 2 percent a year, an increase that nonetheless permitted better pay, more recruits and ones of much higher quality, and improved reenlistment rates. Operation and maintenance did even better, averaging a 6.2 percent annual real increase that permitted improvements in living conditions, more training, somewhat greater readiness in a slightly larger force, and growth in war reserve stocks.[8] As more new equipment came into the inventory, the assumption was that both accounts would expand much more rapidly.

Fiscal 1986–89

Unfortunately, both this certainty of rapid expansion and several other assumptions about the defense budget proved wrong. By 1985 public and congressional concerns about the related problems of the trade and federal budget deficits and about waste and mismanagement of the defense buildup had manifested themselves, new leadership had appeared in the Soviet Union, and the defense budget had become a target not for real growth but for real decreases. Over the next four years, defense budget authority fell overall by nearly 11 percent in real terms, and while outlays continued

8. *National Defense Budget Estimates for FY1988–1989*, table 6-8.

to rise through fiscal 1987, they retreated nearly 4 percent by fiscal 1989 (table 2). Indeed, it would now appear that fiscal 1985 was the height of the latest defense boom.

Despite these trends, Secretary of Defense Caspar W. Weinberger continued to fight until his resignation in November 1987 for substantial real increases in the defense budget. He considered additional growth necessary not only for the continued modernization of forces with the current generation of weapons, but also for the early introduction of yet another generation with even more sophisticated and costly capabilities. The five-year defense program he introduced for fiscal 1986–90 probably reflected the true costs of this policy; it required an average annual real increase in budget authority of 6.6 percent and would have expanded defense authority in fiscal 1990 to almost $480 billion (table 3). In 1987, after Congress had rejected this ambitious plan, Weinberger recommended a new five-year plan for fiscal 1987–91 that projected an average real growth of just above 3 percent a year. After the stock market crash of 1987 and Weinberger's departure from office, President Reagan and Congress agreed on budgets for fiscal 1988 and 1989 that attempted to keep defense at its fiscal 1987 level in real terms.[9]

During this four-year struggle the procurement account incurred the greatest percentage reduction of any defense budget item, largely because a few minor programs were canceled, acquisitions were stretched out, and other procurement, the category that includes spare parts, support equipment, and ammunition, was cut. However, funding for research, development, testing, and evaluation, where the next generation of weapons was coming to maturity, increased 5.1 percent in real terms (table 2). Meanwhile, funding for military personnel rose by 2.4 percent in real terms and operation and maintenance actually declined by 2 percent.

Into the 1990s

It would be difficult to say that a coherent program has emerged from the trials of the past four years. Consequently the Bush administration will have to face a number of unpalatable facts as it prepares its own five-year program for fiscal 1990–94 and tries to put the defense house in order. Not the least of these facts is that owing to the emphasis on investment in the Reagan budgets and the lag between the appropriation of

9. *Department of Defense Annual Report, Fiscal Year 1989*, pp. 124–25.

Table 2. Department of Defense Budget Authority, by Appropriation Title, Fiscal Years 1985–89

Billions of fiscal 1990 dollars unless otherwise specified

Title	1985	1986	1987	1988	1989	Percent real change 1985–89
Authority						
Military personnel	78.1	75.4[a]	80.4	80.2	80.0	2.4
Operation and maintenance	91.1	86.7	89.2	88.6	89.3	−1.9
Procurement	113.6	105.2	88.3	85.1	81.5	−28.3
Research, development, test, and evaluation	36.9	38.5	39.6	39.1	38.8	5.1
Military construction	6.5	6.1	5.6	5.7	5.9	−9.2
Family housing	3.4	3.2	3.4	3.4	3.4	0
Other[b]	6.1	5.9	2.7	0.9	0.4	c
Total	335.7	321.0	309.2	303.0	299.3	−10.8
Outlays	286.1	302.8	304.3	297.3	293.9	2.7

Sources: *Department of Defense Annual Report, Fiscal Year 1990*, pp. 83, 89, 219; and William W. Kaufmann, "A Defense Agenda for Fiscal Years 1990–1994," in John D. Steinbruner, ed., *Restructuring American Foreign Policy* (Brookings, 1988), p. 57.

a. Lower budget authority in fiscal 1986 resulted from congressional direction to finance $4.5 billion for military pay raises and retirement accrual costs from unobligated balances of budget authority from prior years.

b. Special foreign currency program, revolving and management funds, and trust funds, receipts, and accruals.

c. Year-to-year variations make percentage meaningless.

budget authority and its actual spending, large balances of budget authority remain from prior years and will have an impact on future defense spending regardless of what new budget authority may be appropriated (table 4). Thus if the level of defense spending is to help reduce the federal deficit and these prior-year balances are left untouched, control of future outlays will depend heavily on how much of what kinds of new budget authority is appropriated. A strategy that strongly emphasizes long-term investments at the expense of current operations and support will reduce near-term expenditures but ensure much higher longer-term costs. A preference for maintaining current readiness and sustainability, combined with a more modest program of investments will mean fewer savings in the first several years of a five-year program but a rapid increase in savings thereafter. In theory, it is also possible to cancel contracts and rescind prior-year authority. However, P.L. 99-177, the Gramm-Rudman-Hollings deficit reduction law, bans any congressional rescission of obligated authority, and the Defense Department has been notoriously reluctant to cancel contracts on its own, particularly because of the penalties associated with such action.[10]

10. Kaufmann, "Defense Agenda," pp. 49–51.

Table 3. Five-Year Defense Plans, Fiscal Years 1986–90, 1987–91, 1988–92
Billions of current dollars unless otherwise specified

Period	1986	1987	1988	1989	1990	1991	1992	Percent average estimated annual real growth
Budget authority								
1986–90	313.7	354.0	401.6	438.8	477.7	. . .	. . .	6.6
1987–91	. . .	311.6	332.4	353.5	374.7	395.5	. . .	3.1
1988–92	. . .	. . .	303.3	323.3	343.9	364.9	386.5	3.0
Outlays								
1986–90	277.5	312.3	348.6	382.3	418.3	. . .	. . .	6.8
1987–91	. . .	274.3	290.7	313.3	335.5	356.6	. . .	3.3
1988–92	. . .	. . .	289.3	303.7	321.0	340.0	361.0	2.1

Sources: *Department of Defense Annual Report, Fiscal Year 1986*, pp. 71, 78, 239; *Budget of the United States Government, Fiscal Year 1987*, pp. 6e-12, 6e-18; *Department of Defense Annual Report, Fiscal Year 1987*, pp. 101, 313; *Department of Defense Annual Report, Fiscal Year 1988*, pp. 86, 98, 327; and *Budget of the United States Government, Fiscal Year 1988*, pp. 5-12, 5-15.

Another stark possibility is that unless severe constraints are placed on the investment accounts, continuing to buy the current generation of weapons and acquiring the next generation of systems now under development could cost $1 trillion (table 5). On top of that amount, if the past is any precedent, operating and support funds would have to increase proportionately if the armed forces are to maintain an acceptable level of readiness and sustainability. It is little wonder then that in the circumstances Secretary Weinberger foresaw the need for average real increases in budget authority of 7 percent a year and a fiscal 1986-90 defense program of $2 trillion.

On the other side of the ledger, Congress has been cutting defense budget authority by an average of 2.8 percent a year in real terms for the past four years and for fiscal 1986–90 has authorized only $1.5 trillion.[11] Exactly what its targets will be for the next five years is not yet certain, but the best that the Defense Department can probably hope for is a real freeze, a budget that will grow only by the amount of inflation. Equally possible is that Congress will adopt a recommendation of the Democratic Study Group and impose limits approximating a nominal freeze, which would mean that budget authority (or expenditures) would remain at the current level and would actually decline by the rate of inflation, estimated by the Pentagon (on the optimistic side) as averaging 2.5 percent a year between 1990 and 1994.[12]

11. *Department of Defense Annual Report, Fiscal Year 1989*, table 1.

12. The Report of the Democratic Study Group is summarized in *Inside the Pentagon*, December 16, 1988, p. 5. For the estimate of inflation see *Department of Defense Annual Report, Fiscal Year 1990*, pp. 89, 219.

8   *William W. Kaufmann and Lawrence J. Korb*

Table 4. Balances of Budget Authority for Defense and Energy from Prior Years, Fiscal Years 1988–90
Billions of current dollars

	Start 1988	End 1988	End 1989	End 1990
Defense				
Obligated	212.5	216.9	218.4	227.7
Unobligated	47.6	42.3	41.2	43.6
Energy				
Obligated	7.2	6.9	7.8	8.1
Unobligated	2.0	1.8	1.1	1.4
Total	269.3	267.9	268.5	280.8

Source: *Budget of the United States Government, Fiscal Year 1990*, p. 10-18.

The import of these facts and probabilities is unlikely to escape the attention of the planners in the Bush administration: barring an act of God or a major increase in taxes, a gap will grow between the programs that defense has on its books and the resources likely to be made available to it during the next five years. Somewhere, somehow, something will have to give. The issue is clear; the appropriate choice is a good deal less so.

Certain other data are, or should be, of some relevance to the choices that the Bush administration faces. First, by historical peacetime standards, the level of defense spending is very high. In the 1950s, peacetime budgets averaged $202 billion a year in constant fiscal 1989 dollars; in the 1960s they averaged $224 billion and in the 1970s only $206 billion (table 6). The average for the 1980s was $292 billion, slightly below the request for fiscal 1990. Second, even after four years of real reductions, defense spending today (in constant dollars) is higher than at the peak of the Vietnam War and more than 50 percent higher than the post-Vietnam War low of fiscal 1975. Thus, the problem that Bush faces is not so much the amount of money available to the Defense Department but rather that the amount is far lower than Reagan and Weinberger anticipated in their programs a few short years ago.

The Context of Choice

The context within which defense spending choices will have to be made can suggest the general direction in which it makes sense for the United States to go. Worth stressing at the outset is the fact that the U.S.

Table 5. Estimated Cost of Equipment in the Defense Pipeline, Fiscal Years 1990–99
Billions of current dollars

Component	Cost
Army	
Aircraft and helicopter	15.6
Tactical missiles	27.2
Tracked vehicles	20.0
Other procurement	29.6
National Guard and reserve equipment	9.3
Subtotal	101.7
Navy	
Aircraft and helicopters	141.8
Shipbuilding and conversion	107.9
Missiles and torpedoes	70.6
Other procurement	15.2
Marine Corps (ground equipment only)	2.6
Subtotal	338.1
Air Force	
Space	24.0
Aircraft and strategic missiles	306.5
Tactical missiles	22.5
Other procurement	46.6
Subtotal	399.6
General	
Strategic defense initiative	119.3
Classified programs	48.9
Total	1,007.6

Sources: Kaufmann, "Defense Agenda," p. 83; *Armed Forces Journal International*, December 1988, pp. 30, 34, and February 1989, p. 16; *Military Forum*, January–February 1989, p. 28; *Defense News*, February 13, 1989, p. 10; and author estimates.

economy could readily provide for a greatly expanded defense. As former Secretary of Defense Frank Carlucci has recently pointed out, defense spending is a relatively modest 5.6 percent of GNP.[13] Thus the issue, at least in part, is not ability to pay but the willingness of the American taxpayers to sacrifice other goods and services to provide for more defense. At present they show no such willingness; indeed, most opinion polls indicate that 84 percent believe defense spending, even after four years of real reductions, is about right or too high.[14]

There are other reasons for moderating defense expenditures and changing the allocation of whatever resources do become available. Among the

13. Frank C. Carlucci, "No Time To Change U.S. Defense Policy," *New York Times*, January 27, 1989, p. 31.

14. Americans Talk Security, "The Military Budget and Public Opinion," press summary, February 16, 1989.

Table 6. Trends in Defense Budget Authority, Fiscal Years 1951–90
Billions of fiscal 1989 dollars

Year	Authority	Year	Authority
1951	277	1971	226
1952	362	1972	219
1953	298	1973	209
1954	218	1974	201
1955	190	1975	194
1956	193	1976	202
1957	202	1977	212
1958	198	1978	209
1959	210	1979	209
1960	203	1980	213
1961	204	1981	240
1962	235	1982	268
1963	237	1983	289
1964	227	1984	303
1965	218	1985	326
1966	261	1986	312
1967	285	1987	302
1968	289	1988	293
1969	278	1989	291
1970	251	1990	297

Non-war-year average
1954–60	202
1961–65	224
1973–80	206
1981–90	292

Sources: Office of the Assistant Secretary of Defense, *National Defense Budget Estimates for FY 1989–1990*, pp. 61–66; and Lawrence Korb and Stephen Daggett, "The Defense Budget and Strategic Planning," in Joseph Kruzel, ed., *American Defense Annual, 1988–89* (Lexington, Mass.: Lexington Books, 1988), p. 45.

more powerful is President Bush's commitment, at least for now, to a "flexible freeze" in federal spending that for defense spending means zero real growth, some reallocation of resources within the rest of the budget, and no tax increases.[15] And the president maintains a somewhat elastic commitment to the Gramm-Rudman-Hollings law, which requires the federal budget to be in balance by 1993. In these circumstances, and given congressional reluctance to reduce other parts of the federal budget, increases in defense spending would prove unacceptable or would bring about a sequestration order that would cut the budget to the mandated level and would leave defense in even worse shape, since defense spending

15. George Bush, *Building a Better America,* supplement of message to Joint Session of Congress, February 9, 1989, pp. 17–27.

would have to bear half of the total cuts and the reductions would apply equally in percentage terms to all accounts left unprotected by the president.[16]

These considerations apart, it would be hard to argue that the Defense Department has excelled in managing those funds it has received. Particularly in the first half of the 1980s, it was overwhelmed by what amounted to wartime resources without having had to fight a war. Waste, fraud, and abuse were bound to occur when there was so much money to spend and so few controls on how it was spent. As table 7 shows, nine major systems were procured at well below the minimum economical production rate even at the height of the defense buildup. For some time now, a respite from such an indiscriminate process has seemed in order.

Such a respite seems particularly appropriate in light of events and expected changes in the international environment. The signing of the Intermediate-Range Nuclear Forces Treaty, the Soviet withdrawal from Afghanistan, the end of the Iran-Iraq war, the apparent settlement of several other regional conflicts, and the Soviet and East German promises unilaterally to reduce their conventional forces suggest that a basic shift may be taking place in world affairs. Soviet-American relations in particular may be entering an entirely new phase. The enemy on which so much of U.S. force planning has depended could, like the Cheshire cat, be disappearing before Western eyes.

Whether only the smile will be left remains to be seen. Meanwhile, despite justifiable optimism, the case against radical surgery on U.S. forces and defense budgets continues to be strong. The resumption of real growth is not feasible and is probably not necessary after the huge buildup of the 1980s, but expectations of reductions in U.S. overseas deployments, major cuts in forces, or deep slashes in the defense budget are premature. Mikhail Gorbachev's tenure and power remain highly uncertain, and despite his promises the Soviet Union retains very powerful nuclear and conventional forces. The conditions of U.S. security have not changed: Western Europe, Northeast Asia, the Persian Gulf, and the Caribbean still fall within the U.S. defense perimeter. The United States itself remains potentially vulnerable to attack. And the Soviet Union aside, dangers can still arise from unresolved regional tensions and from terrorism, insurgencies, and the proliferation of both nuclear and conventional technologies.

Ways to reduce the U.S. defense burden without creating new instabilities may materialize, but it is well to remember that arms control

16. Kaufmann, "Defense Agenda," pp. 50–51.

Table 7. Weapons Procured at Less Than Minimum Economical Production Rates, Fiscal Years 1983–87

Weapon system	Minimum annual economical rate	Average annual procurement rate
AV-8B aircraft	36	34
F-15 aircraft	120	41
Harpoon missile	360	284
MX missile	21	17
HARM missile	3,240	1,460
IIR Maverick missile	6,000	2,205
TOW-2 missile	21,600	15,482
UH-60 Blackhawk helicopter	96	85
Tomahawk cruise missile	300	186

Source: Congressional Budget Office, *Effects of Weapons Procurement Stretch-Outs on Costs and Schedules* (November 1987), p. 11.

agreements are as likely to be long in coming and short on saving money as they have been in the past. Indeed, some agreements may actually suggest higher defense spending. To insist that the allies bear more of the cost of maintaining U.S. forces on their soil is surely not unreasonable. But to pretend that the United States is not the linchpin of the collective security system or that some condominium of other powers can take its place is unreasonable in the extreme. The simple truth is that no one else can play the American role for the foreseeable future. The basic choice even in the 1990s remains U.S. leadership or international anarchy.

However, to make the case for continued U.S. military strength is not to argue that everything must remain as it is. Despite budgetary constraints, the United States still needs major forces that are modern, ready, mobile, and sustainable. At the same time, the future seems to call for hedging against uncertainty while retaining the flexibility to adapt forces and programs to changing conditions and trends. That, indeed, is the challenge of the coming decade for the Bush administration.

The Carlucci Response to the Challenge

Before outlining the specific steps that President Bush and Defense Secretary Richard Cheney might take to adjust the defense program to the projected budget levels and the changing international environment, it is necessary to assess the impact of Frank C. Carlucci, the second secretary of defense in the Reagan administration, on the defense program and budget. Although Carlucci served as secretary for little more than a year, he had a significant opportunity to affect this nation's international security posture because he was responsible for formulating the Reagan administration's fiscal 1989 and 1990 defense budget requests and the 1990–94 defense program.

The magnitude of the problem Carlucci faced is indicated in table 8, which shows that between 1985 and 1987 the Department of Defense reduced substantially its estimate of the amount of budget authority that would become available in fiscal 1986–90. In early 1985, before the passage of the Gramm-Rudman-Hollings Act, the Pentagon's civilian leadership assumed defense would receive almost $2 trillion in the period. Two years later it recognized that at most it would get $1.5 trillion. However, because of Secretary Weinberger's insistence that the downturn would be only temporary, the department was not allowed to adjust its goals for force structure or slow the pace of modernization. It is no exaggeration to say that Carlucci inherited a $400-billion-a-year program and a $300-billion-a-year budget.

Carlucci's success in reconciling the defense program and budget was mixed. He started well: by February 1988 he had succeeded in reducing the fiscal 1989–93 projections he inherited by $208 billion, about 11 percent (table 9). However, over the next year, he managed to trim only an additional $20 billion, or 1 percent.

Carlucci's February 1988 and January 1989 plans both assumed real growth of 2 percent a year from fiscal 1990 to 1994. However, in the presidential campaign of 1988, neither Bush nor Michael Dukakis would commit himself to any real growth in the defense budget. In fact, on February 9, 1989, President Bush froze defense spending for fiscal 1990 at fiscal 1989 levels and projected only slight real increases for 1991–93.[17] Yet Carlucci insisted until the day he left office that defense could and should receive the full 2 percent real growth; in fact, he continued to lobby for it after he left office.

If the Pentagon receives enough money to keep pace with inflation in fiscal 1990–94—the best it can hope for—total budget authority will have to be cut by another $100 billion (table 10). Zero nominal growth would mean that the Defense Department would have to reduce its projected level of spending by $230 billion.

Adjusting the defense budget is comparatively easy; adjusting the program to conform to that reality is much more complex. In fact the Pen-

17. Bush, *Building a Better America*, p. 138.

Table 8. Department of Defense Five-Year Plans for Fiscal Years 1986–90
Budget authority in billions of current dollars

Plan	1986	1987	1988	1989	1990	Total
Administration request, February 1985	314	354	402	439	478	1,987
Administration request, February 1986	281	312	332	354	375	1,654
Administration request, January 1987	281	282	303	323	344	1,533
Actual authorized	281	279	284	290	306[a]	1,440

Sources: *Department of Defense Annual Report, Fiscal Years 1986, 1987, 1988.*
a. Estimated.

tagon's plan was so far removed from plausible budgetary constraints that it was not produced in 1987 and 1988.[18] The question, then, is whether Carlucci's reductions were programmatic or simply budgetary. Is the fiscal 1989-94 program still significantly underfunded even if the defense budget grows by 2 percent a year in real terms?

In approaching his task of reducing the projected fiscal 1989 defense budget by $33 billion and the fiscal 1989-93 program by $207 billion, Carlucci established reasonably clear priorities. In memoranda issued shortly after he took office, he instructed the services to achieve the necessary reductions by terminating programs, cutting force structure and personnel, and deferring new programs. The armed services were cautioned not to reduce budgets by the time-honored but wasteful practice of simply stretching out programs. The highest priorities, Carlucci said in releasing his fiscal 1989 and 1990 budgets, were quality people, readiness, and efficient acquisition.[19]

In the fiscal 1989 budget Carlucci terminated seventeen programs for a total savings of $4.8 billion in 1989 and $51.7 billion in the 1990s (table 11). However, 45 percent of the savings in 1989 and 77 percent of the total savings were projected to come from one program, the Midgetman land-based small mobile missile, a program favored by the Democratically

18. Lawrence J. Korb, "Spending Without Strategy: The FY 1988 Annual Defense Department Report," *International Security*, vol. 12 (Summer 1987), p. 172; and Cheryl Pellerin, "Nunn Sees Defense Cuts of $325 Billion," *Defense News*, October 24, 1988, p. 1.

19. Paul Mann, "Taft Memos Order Budget Cuts, Emphasize Weapons Terminations," *Aviation Week and Space Technology*, December 7, 1987, pp. 24–26; Office of Assistant Secretary of Defense (Public Affairs), "Amended FY 1988/FY 1989 Department of Defense Budget," press release, February 18, 1988; and Office of Assistant Secretary of Defense (Public Affairs), "FY1990/FY1991 Department of Defense Budget," press release 1-89, January 9, 1989. Unless otherwise noted, information in the next five paragraphs is from these press releases.

Table 9. Department of Defense Five-Year Plans for Fiscal Years 1989–93
Budget authority in billions of current dollars

Plan	1989	1990	1991	1992	1993	Total
Weinberger plan, January 1987	323	344	365	387	413	1,832
Carlucci plan, February 1988	291	307	324	342	360	1,624
Carlucci plan, January 1989	290	306	321	336	351	1,604
Difference, January 1987–February 1988	32	37	41	45	53	208
Difference, January 1987–January 1989	33	38	44	51	62	228

Sources: Office of the Assistant Secretary of Defense (Public Affairs), "FY 1990/FY 1991 Department of Defense Budget," press release 1-89, January 9, 1989; and *Department of Defense Annual Report, Fiscal Year 1988.*

controlled Congress. None of the others was significant in either strategic or monetary terms. Carlucci also deferred or slowed down the planned pace of nine ongoing programs, which resulted in cost deferrals of $1.05 billion in fiscal 1989 (table 11). Finally, he delayed the start of eight programs for a total savings of $441 million. Of the seventeen programs deferred or delayed, only the LHX (light helicopter, experimental), the MK-48 torpedo, and the B-1B bomber enhancements have much budgetary significance. Although delaying them will save money in the short term, they will inevitably cost more in the long term if the planned number of units is finally procured. The Defense Department still spent $850 million on these programs in fiscal 1989, and costs for 1989–91 will rise to $2.78 billion (table 12).

Carlucci claimed to have continued his original priorities in the fiscal 1990–94 program. In January 1989 he canceled an unspecified number of programs and delayed the start of another thirteen beyond 1990–91.

Table 10. Department of Defense Budget Authority, Fiscal Years 1990–94
Billions of current dollars

Plan	1989 base	1990	1991	1992	1993	1994
January 1989	290	306	321	336	351	366
Flat in real terms	290	299	308	316	323	330
Flat in nominal terms	290	290	290	290	290	290
Cumulative shortfall						
Flat in real terms	. . .	7	20	40	68	104
Flat in nominal terms	. . .	16	47	93	154	230

Sources: *Department of Defense Annual Report, Fiscal Year 1990*, p. 89; and author estimates.

erycannot

Table 11. Projected Savings from Defense Program Terminations and Deferrals, Fiscal Year 1989 and Beyond
Millions of current dollars

Service	Program	Savings[a] 1989	1989 and beyond
Terminations			
Army	Aquila remotely piloted vehicle	226	1,096
	Antitactical missile	35	149
	EH-60 helicopter	45	45
	M198 howitzer	20	91
	120mm mortar	24	161
	Copperhead artillery shell	106	747
	Subtotal	455	2,289
Navy	A-6F aircraft	918	5,655
	Navy airship	62	135
	Antiradiation seeker	8	109
	High-frequency antijam (HFAJ) radio	52	87
	Skipper II guided missile	37	209
	Subtotal	1,077	6,194
Air Force	Antisatellite (ASAT) program	786	2,218
	Midgetman missile	2,150	39,790
	Minuteman III penetration aids	129	561
	C-27 aircraft	65	65
	AGM-130 air-to-ground missile	92	401
	Airborne command post replacement	14	140
	Subtotal	3,237	43,175
	Total	4,769	51,658
Deferrals			
Army	Forward area air defense	128	...
	Advanced antiarmor weapons–heavy	92	...
	Armored family of vehicles	45	...
	LHX helicopter restructure	407	...
	Army data distribution system	86	...
Navy	Advanced air-to-air missile	57	...
	MK-48 torpedo	113	...
	MK-50 torpedo	80	...
	Vertical launch air-to-surface rocket	45	...
	Total	1,050	...

Sources: Office of the Assistant Secretary of Defense (Public Affairs), "Amended FY 1988/FY 1989 Department of Defense Budget," press release 81-88, February 18, 1988; and *Budget of the United States Government, Fiscal Year 1990*, p. 10-18.

a. Columns may not add up because of rounding.

However, none was considered significant enough to be listed in the *Department of Defense Annual Report* for 1989.

He also proposed various minor manpower and force structure changes in the fiscal 1989 budget and carried them forward through 1990. In early

Table 12. Projected Cost of Major Deferred Programs, Fiscal Years 1989–91
Millions of current dollars

Program	1989	1990	1991	Total
LHX helicopter	124	241	447	812
MK-48 torpedo	481	501	412	1,394
B1-B bomber	243	132	194	569
Total	848	874	1,053.	2,775

Source: *Department of Defense Annual Report, Fiscal Year 1990*, pp. 135, 152, 190.

1987 the Defense Department had assumed that its total force strength in 1989 would be 4,522,000 active-duty personnel, selected reserves, and direct-hire civilians. In his fiscal 1989 budget request, Carlucci reduced the number on the payroll to 4,413,000 by cutting 46,000 active-duty military personnel, 40,000 selected reserves, and 23,000 civilians. His fiscal 1990 and 1991 budgets left these strengths virtually the same. The manpower savings will cut $3.2 billion from the projected defense payroll in fiscal 1989 and another $4.2 billion in 1990. Of the reductions in force structure in the fiscal 1989–93 program, the most significant were the deletion of one active Army brigade and two Air Force tactical air wings and the retirement of sixteen older Navy frigates. These changes should save about $2 billion a year in operating costs between fiscal 1989 and 1994.

Even though Carlucci made readiness his highest priority, he allowed some diminution of readiness and sustainability for each of the services in his two budget exercises. The operating tempos or training rates of Army tank units were cut by 6 percent from 850 tank miles a year to 800, while Army helicopter flying time is still at its 1980 level and well below the objective of the service. The Army also suffered a decline in munitions sustainability. Since 1987 the Navy has annually deferred the overhaul of four ships because of a lack of funds, and this practice is likely to persist over the next few years. Finally, the Air Force accrued a significant shortfall in war reserve materiel, particularly spare parts.[20]

Table 13, which compares Carlucci's fiscal 1989, 1990, and 1991 budgets with the fiscal 1989 projections inherited from Secretary Weinberger, shows that Carlucci succeeded in slightly altering the budget priorities of his predecessor. By fiscal 1991, when nominal defense spending will have returned to its projected 1989 level, Carlucci's changes will have shifted about $5 billion from investment into readiness (personnel and maintenance). Thus he appears to have followed through on his pledge to emphasize the readiness of the current force more than modernization.

20. *Department of Defense Annual Report, Fiscal Year 1990*, p. 129, 143, 160.

Table 13. Defense Budgets, by Program Category, Fiscal Years 1989–91
Billions of current dollars

Category	1989 request[a]	1989 revised[b]	1990 request	1991 proposed
Military personnel	81.6	78.6	79.8	82.1
Operation and maintenance	91.5	85.9	91.7	95.5
Procurement	94.6	80.0	84.1	91.9
Readiness	27.1	23.1	23.0	25.1
Modernization	67.5	56.9	61.1	66.8
Research, development, test, and evaluation	44.3	37.5	41.0	41.3
Military construction	10.6	9.0	8.6	9.6
Total	322.6	290.2	305.2	320.4

Sources: *Department of Defense Annual Report, Fiscal Year 1990*, p. 219; Lawrence J. Korb and Stephen Daggett, "The Defense Budget and Strategic Planning on a New Plateau," in Daggett and others, *The Military Budget on a New Plateau: Strategic Choices for the 1990s* (Washington: Committee for National Security, 1988), p. 19; and Office of Assistant Secretary of Defense (Public Affairs), "Amended FY 1988/FY 1989 Department of Defense Budget," News Release 81-88, February 18, 1988.
a. Submitted in January 1987 as part of a biennial fiscal year 1988–89 budget.
b. Submitted in February 1988.

However, this shift only holds true if one looks at the procurement account as a whole. If procurement is broken into its two components, readiness and modernization, a different picture emerges: items critical to readiness—spare parts, munitions, support equipment—are acquired in this account along with major systems such as planes, ships, tanks, and strategic missiles. After assuming office, Carlucci treated major systems or modernization procurement much more favorably than readiness procurement (table 13). He cut both by about 15 percent in his first submission, but for fiscal 1990, he increased spending for the big-ticket items by 7 percent while leaving readiness procurement essentially flat. And his 1991 projection widens the disparity even more by proposing a 13 percent increase in modernization and 9 percent for readiness procurement.

While Carlucci's choices pointed U.S. defense in the right direction, he did little to ameliorate the Pentagon's long-term budget problems. The military still has a force structure that is either too large for adequate budgetary support or one that is being modernized too quickly. Indeed, the five-year defense plan Carlucci left behind still shows $45 billion in unitemized subtractions. These "negative funding wedges" are labeled program estimates and must be specified and approved by Congress if defense is to grow at no more than 2 percent a year from 1990 to 1994.[21]

21. "Cuts That Don't Hurt," *National Journal*, February 4, 1989, p. 269.

To add to the problems, the economic assumptions underlying the projected five-year defense plan are unrealistic. In the budgets for fiscal 1990–94, defense "saves" $31 billion at its 2 percent real growth level simply by changing some of the prices upon which the budget is based (table 14). If oil prices do not fall by 10.3 percent in fiscal 1990, if civilian pay raises do not stay at 2 percent, and if inflation does not stay at 3.6 percent, the Pentagon will have an even more serious problem as it tries to reconcile its program with its budget. One defense publication called the fiscal 1990 defense request "unrealistic at its core."[22] If the assumptions underlying the current five-year plan prove too optimistic and if a nominal freeze is imposed, the Defense Department could be forced to find $410 billion in program cuts over the next five years (table 14). Even if the department receives enough funding to keep pace with inflation and the economy performs much better than expected, its program would still be underfunded by $150 billion over the next five years.[23] Reductions of that magnitude in the proposed fiscal 1990-94 program, coming on top of about $500 billion in reductions to the projected fiscal 1986-90 program, should entail dramatic changes in defense planning.

A More Flexible Response

Whatever else may be said, one aspect of Carlucci's response to the challenge of the future was almost certainly unrealistic: Congress will not appropriate a 2 percent real increase in defense budget authority as long as President Bush refuses to raise taxes, other national needs are assuming increased importance, and the president's highest priority is to reduce the federal budget deficit. Indeed Mr. Bush has already ordered the Pentagon to freeze defense authority for fiscal 1990 at its 1989 level in real terms and has limited increases in the following three years to 1 percent, 1 percent, and 2 percent (table 15).

Modernization

Despite these new constraints, a more serious problem for the longer term has been the failure to develop a coherent, consistent policy on the

22. "Weapons Summit," *Aviation Week and Space Technology*, January 16, 1989, p. 7.
23. Congressional Budget Office, *Reducing the Deficit: Spending and Revenue Options*, pt. 2 (March 1988), table 1.

Table 14. Defense Budget Projections and Potential Shortfall in Program Support, Fiscal Years 1990–94

Billions of current dollars

Projections	1990	1991	1992	1993	1994
February 1988					
(Carlucci plan)	307	324	342	360	378
January 1989					
(Carlucci plan)	306	321	336	351	366
Cumulative difference	1	4	10	19	31
Cumulative potential shortfall of					
1989 plan	24	71	158	271	410
Component:					
Inflation greater than expected	1	4	10	19	31
Unitemized subtractions (funding					
wedges) included	0	0	15	30	45
Effects of real freeze	7	20	40	68	104
Effects of nominal freeze	16	47	93	154	230

Sources: *Department of Defense Annual Report, Fiscal Year 1989* and *Fiscal Year 1990*; and author projections.

modernization of the armed forces. Owing to the munificent funding of the early 1980s and the expectation that it would continue, the armed services engaged in an uncoordinated, redundant scramble to develop and deploy wholly new systems even before the current wave of modernization had been completed. And the scramble has continued despite the real decreases in the defense budget. As one consequence, the Pentagon is running up an enormous investment bill that, before being paid in full, will crowd out even the needs of the operating and support accounts unless

Table 15. Carlucci and Bush Budget Authority and Outlay Projections, Fiscal Years 1989–93

Billions of current dollars

Item	1989	1990	1991	1992	1993	Total difference
Authority						
Carlucci (1989)	290.2	305.6	320.9	335.7	350.7	. . .
Bush	290.2	299.3	311.0	322.0	335.9	. . .
Difference	0	6.3	9.9	13.7	14.8	44.7
Outlays						
Carlucci (1989)	289.8	293.8	304.7	316.2	329.3	. . .
Bush	289.8	291.2	298.8	306.8	317.4	. . .
Difference	0	2.6	5.9	9.4	11.9	29.8

Sources: *Department of Defense Annual Report, Fiscal Year 1990*, pp. 83, 89; and George Bush, *Building a Better America*, February 9, 1989, p. 139.

future budgets are afforded annual real increases much higher than the 2 percent requested by Carlucci.

Apart from instituting more centralized and disciplined planning, the Pentagon must recognize that modernization need not entail wholesale change. Modernization consists of two basic components. The first concerns changes in the launching platforms—aircraft, ships, tracked vehicles, and so forth—from which the warheads, bullets, tactical missiles, and other munitions are fired. The second encompasses the munitions themselves and all the subsystems associated with their reliable and accurate delivery to designated targets. Thus if platforms are appropriately designed, modernization need not (and in practice does not) require the introduction of entirely new systems at relatively short intervals.

Since World War II, in fact, the United States has rolled over its inventory of platforms approximately every two decades—the Trident submarine came along twenty years after the Polaris, the F-15 fighter twenty years after the F-4, and the M-1 tank twenty years after the M-60—without any major failures of deterrence or any sacrifice of performance in combat operations. This history, combined with the technological advantages that the United States and its allies maintain over potential enemies, suggests that despite recurrent alarms about bomber and missile gaps or windows of vulnerability, despite fears of failing to field new weapons quickly enough, changes in the basic inventory of platforms should be slowed rather than accelerated. Claims to the contrary notwithstanding, U.S. defense appears to be keeping up with the Soviet Union. For at least another five years America could accomplish more with the same amount of funds by upgrading current platforms through improving subsystems than by rushing to replace them, especially since more significant technological changes appear to be taking place in munitions and subsystems than in platform design.

In addition to continuing to replace platforms only every twenty years or so, it probably makes sense to design new systems with attention to realistic cost constraints instead of trying to satisfy stringent performance requirements that are as likely to be based on what U.S. technology might be capable of accomplishing as on sober estimates of evolving threats. Exactly what the costs should be undoubtedly will have to vary with the individual system. However, if it is assumed that in peacetime—as has been the case with both the Soviet Union and the United States over the past forty-five years—defense budgets will increase in real terms by an average 3 percent a year because of technological improvements and increased operating and support costs, a next generation of systems should cost no more than twice its predecessor in constant dollars. Thus if a B-52 were to cost about $130 million in current prices, its successor should be designed to cost no more than $260 million, or slightly less than the price of the B-1B.

Such an approach would ensure greater predictability in the budget process and give system designers more freedom to envision the best possible performance within a known cost constraint. It would also allow ample time for prototyping, testing, and evaluating new systems before going into production and would minimize the flaws and waste associated with concurrent development and production of systems and subsequent efforts to repair defects by means of extensive changes and retrofits off the production line. Finally, a cost-based approach would help prevent bringing in new systems before the current wave of modernization has been completed and field units have learned to exploit existing technologies.

Strategic Nuclear Forces

Nowhere did the Reagan administration differ more from a cost-based approach than in its efforts to modernize the strategic nuclear forces. It inherited a triad of capabilities (intercontinental ballistic missiles, submarine-launched ballistic missiles, and bombers) that comprised more than 1,800 launchers and 9,000 warheads (table 16). Even after a well-executed Soviet first strike, an all-out U.S. retaliation was expected to deliver some 3,000 warheads to a wide range of targets in the Soviet Union. In addition, the president could withhold certain parts of the force (particularly the SLBMs) and avoid direct attacks on a number of targets, including cities. All in all the deterrent was a powerful one.

Despite the general adequacy of the strategic forces, the Ford and Carter administrations had had three concerns about future capabilities. First, they feared that the land-based ICBMs would become increasingly vulnerable as the Soviet Union improved the accuracy and reliability of its heavy, MIRVed (multiple, independently targetable, reentry vehicles) ICBMs. Second, they expected the B-52 force to experience growing attrition, not because they were older than the pilots who flew them (owing to many upgrades they were not) but because more effective Soviet defenses would find the planes easier to locate, even at low altitudes, and to track and attack. Third, they were concerned about the aging of the

Table 16. Strategic Nuclear Forces, by Type, Fiscal Year 1980

Type	Launchers	Warheads	Second-strike delivered warheads
Offensive			
ICBMs			
Tital II	52	52	11
Minuteman II	450	450	162
Minuteman III	550	1,650	594
Subtotal	1,052	2,152	767
Bombers			
B-52D	75	600	127
B-52G	145	1,740	367
B-52H	96	1,152	243
FB-111	56	336	71
Subtotal	372	3,828	808
Submarine-launched ballistic missiles			
Polaris	80	80	32
Poseidon (C-3 and C-4)	336	3,040	1,459
Subtotal	416	3,120	1,491
Total offensive	1,840	9,100	3,066
Defensive			
Strategic defense interceptors			
Active	127	. . .	. . .
Air National Guard	165	. . .	. . .
Total defensive	292	. . .	. . .

Sources: *Department of Defense Annual Report, Fiscal Year 1989*, p. 313; and author estimates.

ballistic missile submarine force and committed to improving its status as the backbone of the triad.

To deal with these potential inadequacies, the Defense Department (in some cases well before the Ford and Carter administrations) devised various remedies. Two hundred MX missiles, with 2,000 warheads, were to be developed and deployed in a ''racetrack mode'' as a substitute for the ICBM force in its fixed, hardened silos. Some B-52s would be upgraded yet again to improve their penetration capabilities, and others would be armed with the new standoff ALCM (air-launched cruise missile). Plans for the B-1A bomber would be canceled and development would proceed with the stealth (B-2) bomber. The large Trident submarine, with twenty-four launchers instead of sixteen would initially carry the C-4 (Trident I) missile and would eventually be equipped with the much more accurate

D-5 (Trident II) SLBM. Thus all three legs of the triad would be modernized and made less vulnerable, the number of warheads in the force would be increased, and the combination of the MX and D-5 missiles would give the offense an even more impressive prompt, hard-target kill capability than the Minuteman III with its Mark-12A warheads.

The Reagan administration not only adopted most of these measures (the main exception was the racetrack basing mode for the MX missile) but added to them. It proposed to upgrade the Minuteman III and to provide new penetration aids for the Minuteman II. Fifty MX missiles were to be placed in fixed Minuteman silos and another fifty were to sit on trains (the rail garrison MX), ready to dash onto the rails upon receipt of an unspecified kind of warning. At the same time, because of pressure from some members of Congress and its own commission on strategic choices (the Scowcroft Commission), the administration ordered work to begin on a small ICBM (popularly known as Midgetman), which would be mounted on special transporters that would roam military reservations and disperse still further upon warning. The bomber leg of the triad fared equally well. The B-1 bomber was revived as the B-1B and rushed into production. The advanced cruise missile, allegedly with stealth features, proceeded into development as a successor to the air-launched cruise missile (ALCM). Development of the B-2 (stealth) bomber was continued, and the plane made its public debut in late 1988. Only the SLBM force evolved essentially as planned. Even continental air defenses underwent a face-lift with the modernization of the distant early warning line (now known as North Warning), the acquisition of new interceptors, and the deployment of the OTH-B (over-the-horizon–backscatter) radars. The Reagan administration also pursued development of an ASAT (antisatellite) system and, in its most dramatic gesture, the president himself launched the strategic defense initiative (SDI) in March 1983 to make ballistic missiles impotent and obsolete. Indeed, over the next six years Reagan requested more than $26 billion to realize this vision, although an insufficiently enraptured Congress has (for the past five years) appropriated less than 75 percent of the total, not counting the funds that went into a multitude of research programs on directed energy before the president achieved his special vision and consolidated the programs into a single Strategic Defense Initiative Office.[24] The Reagan administration's efforts increased the portion of the defense budget spent directly on strategic forces and

24. "Star Wars' Budget Figure," *New York Times,* January 27, 1989, p. 1.

related research from 11 percent in 1980 to 16 percent in 1985. Actual spending went from $11 billion to $27 billion.

Secretary Carlucci's five-year defense plan appeared to reduce somewhat this scattershot approach to strategic nuclear planning. In a decision unlikely to stand, it ended work on the small ICBM and bowed to Air Force preference for the rail garrison MX. The plan also continued SDI at a rapid pace, but from a lower funding base than the administration had originally envisioned. However, the basic problems of the original Reagan program still remained. Indeed, when Carlucci left office, strategic programs (as defined in the mission budget) continued to consume 14 percent of the defense budget.

Nowhere are problems more evident than in the struggle to modernize the ICBMs. In the past the silo-based force performed at least two valuable functions. It provided a highly survivable, controllable capability that could attack hard as well as soft targets with more than a minimal probability of success. Equally important, it made knocking out both the U.S. alert bombers and the ICBMs extremely difficult if not impossible for an enemy first-strike planner. Even though the value of the first function is now in doubt because of the increasing accuracy of heavy Soviet ICBMs, the silo-based Minuteman force (along with the fifty MXs in fixed silos) is still more than adequate to perform the second function, despite unsubstantiated rumors that the Soviet Union is taking steps to be able to destroy both the ICBMs and alert bombers on the ground.[25] Meanwhile the D-5 (Trident II) missile can provide whatever hard-target kill capability is deemed necessary, even though some may argue speciously that communication difficulties will prevent the prompt use of warheads based on submarines. In the circumstances, it is reasonable to ask why either the rail garrison MX or the small ICBM is needed.

To be sure, there is a considerable and appropriate tradition of wanting to provide extra insurance in the design of the strategic nuclear forces and an understandable desire to deploy offensive forces that, with the exception of the recallable bombers, do not have to depend on warning (with its false alarms) to survive but can ride out an attack and still retaliate as planned. Even today the triad satisfies both requisites, and its continuation is therefore much to be desired—but not at any price. And there lies one of the two high hurdles for both the rail garrison MX and the small ICBM.

25. Brent Scowcroft and R. James Woolsey, "Defense and Arms Control Policy," in *American Agenda: Report to the Forty-First President of the United States*, pt. 3, pp. 2–3.

The MX is cheaper than the Midgetman, but both are expensive.[26] And it remains unclear how much warning either will need if it is to have a high probability of surviving an enemy first strike. At the moment the small ICBM looks better because of its second-strike performance, but neither seems a very good bet for early procurement and deployment, especially when the need for them is questionable and defense funding remains tight.

What is happening in the program to modernize bombers is equally troublesome. The issue is not so much the survivability of alert bombers on the ground as it is their ability to penetrate upgraded and more efficiently operated Soviet air defenses. Clearly, the issue must be faced; but whether it has to be resolved with a rapid sequence of such new penetrating devices as the air-launched cruise missile, the advanced cruise missile, and the B-1B and B-2 bombers is another matter entirely. The Air Force has now worked with the ALCM for ten years; presumably the system is reliable and accurate enough to have a high probability of penetrating Soviet air defenses and destroying fixed targets not already covered by ballistic missiles. The ACM, with its stealth technology, should have a somewhat higher probability of kill and promises to counteract any improvement in Soviet airborne radar used to direct antiaircraft weapons—so-called look-down, shoot-down capabilities—beyond what is reasonable to expect in the coming decade.

What task, then, is left to the manned, penetrating bomber? One possibility is for it to serve as insurance against the failure of the cruise missiles, provided that it is difficult to detect by radar except at short ranges. But bombers are very expensive insurance: in the past eight years 60 percent of the strategic offensive budget has been spent for bombers—at least $28 billion of it on 100 B-1Bs—yet they still have serious flaws as penetrating bombers, flaws that the Congressional Budget Office estimates could cost $8 billion to fix.[27] Rather than continue to repair their defects, the Defense Department might better convert them into the Rolls Royces of cruise missile carriers. The B-2 is even more costly and untried; the Air Force wants 132 of them at a projected price of at least $68 billion, or more than $500 million a copy, but has failed to explain what the B-2 can do that cannot be done more efficiently by ballistic and cruise

---

26. Stephen Daggett and others, *The Military Budget on a New Plateau: Strategic Choices for the 1990s* (Washington: Committee for National Security, 1988), table 9.

27. Molly Moore, "Upgrading B1 Could Cost $8 Billion, Hill Told," *Washington Post,* August 23, 1988, p. A4.

missiles. To proceed with production without adequately defining the B-2's mission or subjecting it to rigorous testing and evaluation would be imprudent at the very least. Indeed, however great the merits of stealth technology, its application to a nuclear bomber likely to be on a one-shot mission seems misplaced. True, it is argued that the B-2 (like the B-52s in Vietnam) could be used on conventional bombing missions, and Air Force officials have contended that it would have been perfect for the 1986 bombing of Libya.[28] But whether use on such missions constitutes a plausible argument in light of the small number of bombers and their high unit cost is open to question. The B-2 may prove a technological marvel, as the RB-70 did in its day, but it too could be an expensive strategic mistake and end up in a museum.

There is, of course, one possibility that cannot be overlooked: that the B-2, the MX, the D-5, the nuclear attack submarine SSN-21 (Seawolf), and a deployed antiballistic missile defense as an outgrowth of SDI could be seen as enabling U.S. strategic forces to destroy all fixed hard targets in the Soviet Union, hunt down land-mobile and submarine-based ballistic missiles, and intercept any warheads that escape the attention of the offense. But if such is the vision, it is defective. Given the prospect of Soviet countermeasures, such a system of offense and defense would not be likely to keep U.S. fatalities low, and it would be difficult, in any event, to persuade an American president otherwise. As President Reagan, despite his advocacy of SDI, said many times, a nuclear war cannot be won and must never be fought.[29] Furthermore, any such vision flatly contradicts the goal of mutual deterrence sought by the United States in the strategic arms reduction talks (START). Whatever the merits of particular proposals in START—and they do deserve serious review—they presumably are intended to ensure that, at lower levels of launchers and warheads, each side will retain a significant and roughly equivalent retaliatory capability.

That goal suggests the strategy and force structure the United States should consider adopting in the 1990s. What has been called in the past a countervailing strategy still seems most appropriate. Such a strategy implies the ability of the United States to reply in kind (but not necessarily in numbers) to any nuclear attack that the Soviet Union might undertake and to halt an exchange before population centers become targets. In other

28. "The Stealth Bomber Won't Breeze by the Budget Boys," *Business Week,* December 12, 1988, p. 76.

29. *Department of Defense Annual Report, Fiscal Year 1986,* p. 45.

words, however unlikely, if the Soviet Union should launch an attack against American missiles and bombers, the United States should have the forces necessary to respond against equivalent targets—to demonstrate that an attempt at a disarming first strike had failed—as well as the communications to withhold other survivable forces so as to offer the opportunity to end the folly.

In principle, a submarine-based ballistic missile force equipped with a modest number of D-5 hard-target killers could satisfy all the conditions of a countervailing strategy. Moreover, such a force would be the cheapest available, measured in the cost of second-strike delivered warheads. However, prudence and uncertainty, particularly with regard to the survivability of submarines, dictate three other broad measures. The first is a continuation of the triad based not only on the SLBMs but also on the current ICBM force and ALCMs aboard B-52 and B-1B bombers. The second is a deferral of any early deployment of such systems as the rail garrison MX, the small ICBM, the B-2 bomber, and large numbers of D-5 SLBMs pending the outcome of the START talks. The third is a research and development program that would hedge against future and unfavorable events by allowing the testing and evaluation of no more than six B-2 bombers, modest funding for the Midgetman (but not for the rail garrison MX), the design of a ballistic missile submarine smaller than the Trident and with fewer launchers, and a level of effort on SDI (including any spinoff for antisatellite systems) that would not exceed $3 billion a year in current dollars for fiscal 1990–94. Table 17 shows that the Carlucci strategic program spending could be reduced by two-thirds if these three measures were adopted. Table 18 summarizes the kind of force that could be deployed under a nominal freeze by the mid-1990s and the number of warheads the force should be able to deliver on Soviet targets in a second strike. From a day-to-day alert (the normal peacetime status of the force), some 3,600 warheads could reach their destinations, a capability more than strong enough to ensure strategic deterrence while helping the Defense Department deal with the budgetary freeze and reducing to its pre-Reagan level the share of the defense budget devoted to strategic forces.[30]

30. Representative Les Aspin (Democrat of Wisconsin), chairman of the House Armed Services Committee, and the Center for Strategic and International Studies (CSIS) recommend severe reductions in the planned level of strategic expenditures. They would freeze spending at the fiscal 1989 levels for the next decade and give funding priority to Midgetman and Trident. George C. Wilson, "Pool Strategic Funds, Aspin Warns," *Washington Post*, January 12, 1989, p. 26; and Molly Moore, "Group Urges Cut in Stealth Bomber Production," *Washington Post*, December 29, 1988, p. 6.

Table 17. Strategic Nuclear Program Savings from a Nominal Freeze, Fiscal Years 1990–94
Billions of current dollars

System	Estimated costs of Carlucci plan	Estimated costs under nominal freeze	Estimated saving
B-1B bomber	3.0	0.5	2.5
B-2 stealth bomber	40.7	3.0	37.7
Advanced cruise missile (ACM)	7.8	7.8	0
Rotary launcher	0.4	0.4	0
SRAM-II short-range attack missile	2.1	0.6	1.5
KC-135R tanker	7.8	6.1	1.7
OTH-B radar	1.1	1.1	0
Minuteman II penetration aids	0.6	0	0.6
Minuteman III upgrades	0.3	0.3	0
Rail garrison MX	21.0	0.5	20.5
Small ICBM (Midgetman)	0	5.0	−5.0
Trident II submarine	8.1	8.1	0
Trident II (D-5) ballistic missile	25.6	8.3	17.3
Antisatellite system (ASAT)	4.0	0.6	3.4
TR-1 surveillance aircraft	0.4	0.4	0
Defense support program	5.3	5.3	0
Global positioning satellite	3.5	3.5	0
Defense meteorological support program	1.8	1.8	0
Strategic defense initiative (SDI)	48.4	15.0	33.4
Total	181.9	68.3	113.6

Sources: Kaufmann, "Defense Agenda," pp. 78, 90–91; and author estimates.

Tactical Nuclear Forces

Since the ratification of the INF Treaty, consideration of the balance of conventional forces, especially those in Europe, has become more fashionable. But even though their focus has shifted, many Europeans continue to hold ambivalent attitudes toward nuclear weapons in general and those based in Europe in particular. They see the systems as a wondrously cheap deterrent to World War III, but they give every indication that they would resist any use of nuclear weapons, even those confined to the battlefield. To what extent this ambivalence undermines deterrence, or would undermine it in the event of a major crisis, has fortunately not been tested.

Table 18. Strategic Nuclear Forces' Performance under a Nominal Budget Freeze, Fiscal Year 1994

Delivery system	Number of launchers	Number of warheads	Alert on-station rate (percent)	Probability of delivery (percent)	Expected number of warheads delivered
B-52 (ALCM)	150	3,000	30	72.0	648
B-1B (ACM)	90	2,520	30	72.0	544
Minuteman II	352	352	90	3.2	10
Minuteman III	350	1,050	90	3.2	30
MX	50	500	90	3.2	14
Poseidon C-3	128	1,280	45	80.0	461
Poseidon C-4	192	1,344	45	80.0	484
Trident C-4	264	1,848	54	80.0	798
Trident D-5	192	1,344	54	80.0	581
Total	1,768	13,238	. . .	. . .	3,570

Sources: Congressional Budget Office, *Modernizing U.S. Strategic Offensive Forces: Costs, Effects, and Alternatives* (November 1987), pp. 81, 82–83, 84–85; and author estimates.

Other influential attitudes have also dogged the structuring of the tactical nuclear forces. One prevalent in West Germany is that nuclear weapons fired from German soil should land on someone else's territory, even though such a launch would almost certainly result in retribution against Germany. Another is that a U.S. president would somehow be more willing to fire weapons from land bases in Europe than from submarines, or silos in the United States, even though most presidents who have thought about the matter doubt that Soviet leaders would care as much about the location of the launcher as they would about the perpetrator of the act. Nonetheless, at least some allied officials remain concerned about the consequences of INF. The treaty, as they see it, has weakened nuclear deterrence because, while it has removed four times more Soviet than U.S. warheads from the area, it has left NATO with an inadequate inventory of nuclear launchers—artillery, short-range missiles, dual-capable aircraft—most of which would aim at targets in West or East Germany. Many of the same officials fear that the treaty represents a first step toward a denuclearized Europe, even though France and the United Kingdom would still have their own nuclear forces.

Of course, if conventional stability could be achieved in central Europe, and could be seen as having been achieved, these nuclear issues might fade into the background. Meanwhile, there is no evidence to suggest that the United States has any intention of withdrawing its remaining nuclear launchers from Europe, even though, with the agreement of the allies, it is reducing somewhat its large stockpile of nuclear weapons located there. The Pentagon has even proposed ways to cover targets in Eastern Europe and the Soviet-based nuclear threats to Western Europe without violating INF. The Army has offered to extend the range of the multiple-launch rocket system (MLRS) or the Lance missile, both already stationed in Europe, but they would require new missiles. Assuming that additional funds became available, the Air Force could be persuaded to build the tactical air-to-surface missile (TASM), tailored to conform to the 500-kilometer limit INF allows short-range missiles. Independently of INF, the Navy continues to move toward its goal of more than 700 Tomahawk land-attack nuclear missiles (TLAM-N) based on ships and submarines that could be in a position to fire at targets in central Europe if and when the order to do so were transmitted.[31] U.S. strategic forces also continue to dedicate 400 SLBM warheads to the coverage of the nuclear threat to Europe. With the Soviet Union's removal of SS-4, SS-5, and SS-20 ballistic missiles—but not the Badger, Blinder, and Backfire medium bombers—some SLBM warheads could be reallocated to other targets and thereby make up for the loss of the Pershing II ballistic missiles and the ground-launched cruise missiles (GLCMs) prohibited by INF. Indeed, reallocation is the most efficient way to relieve whatever fears about the adequacy of whatever allied intermediate-range nuclear forces still exist in West Germany and the other NATO countries. What is more, the reallocation entails no incremental financial cost to the United States and no political pain to the members of the alliance.

Conventional Forces

Judgments about the plans of the Reagan administration for conventional forces are more difficult to make, in part because it remains unclear how far the Soviet Union and its cohorts are prepared to go, unilaterally as well as by negotiation, in reducing their very large ground and tactical air forces. Another difficulty arises from the Reagan administration's refusal to relate U.S. conventional capabilities to any strategy other than the vague concept of horizontal escalation or being able to conduct a worldwide war against the Soviet Union. There has also been talk in the Pentagon and in the Bush White House about engaging in "competitive

---

31. *Department of Defense Annual Report, Fiscal Year 1989*, pp. 242–43.

strategies'' to exploit U.S. strengths and enemy weaknesses, although the reality of defense modernization plans for nuclear or conventional forces has not matched the rhetoric of the competitive strategies' advocates. Indeed once these advocates began to try to change modernization plans, they were met with fierce resistance from the services and the Joint Chiefs of Staff, who convinced the deputy secretary of defense to muzzle them.[32]

Despite this lack of specific guidance, the Joint Chiefs have followed the practice under previous administrations of requesting forces to deal with specific contingencies in conjunction with allies. In the past, at least in the eyes of the Joint Chiefs, that has meant a strategy with five major components:

—forward defense of such critical areas as northern Norway, central Europe, Thrace, the oil states of the Persian Gulf, South Korea, Alaska, Panama, and the Caribbean, but with the option, given the forces generated for these purposes, to use the forces elsewhere as other contingencies arise and the president might direct;

—defense of the four major sea lanes to Europe, the eastern Mediterranean, Northeast Asia, and the Persian Gulf;

—overseas deployment of ground, air, and naval forces to such sensitive and vital areas as Western Europe, the Persian Gulf, South Korea, Alaska, and Panama to support deterrence, provide an initial defense against surprise or short-warning attack, and create foundations for subsequent reinforcements, if they should prove necessary;

—maintenance of the bulk of the U.S. conventional capabilities in the continental United States, along with a capability for rapid deployment to permit a timely response to crises and sudden attacks; and

—subsequent determination of objectives and needs, depending on the evolution of any conflict, and provision of hedge against such needs by means of the National Guard and reserves, the individual ready reserves, a standby draft mechanism, and war reserve stocks for at least sixty days and preferably for six months.

The forces deemed necessary by the Joint Chiefs to execute this strategy were substantial and constituted the objectives that the Reagan administration sought to attain. However, as of the end of fiscal 1988 the forces in place, particularly conventional forces, had fallen far short of these goals (table 19). This shortfall, combined with budget constraints, has raised issues about appropriate force size and composition and future

---

32. David C. Morrison, ''A Pentagon Strategy Draws Flak,'' *National Journal,* December 31, 1988, pp. 3257–58.

Table 19. Joint Chiefs of Staff Objectives for Minimum-Risk Nuclear and Conventional Force Levels, by Type, Fiscal Year 1991

Type	Number required			Number deployed, end of fiscal 1988
	Active-duty	*Reserve*	*Total*	
Nuclear				
ICBMs	1,254	. . .	1,254	1,000
Ballistic missile submarines	44	. . .	44	31
Strategic bombers	483	. . .	483	372
Conventional				
Army divisions	25	8	33	28
Marine amphibious forces (divisions and air wings)	3	1	4	4
Air Force tactical fighter wings	38	19	57	37
Aircraft carrier battle groups	22	. . .	22	14
Intercontinental airlift aircraft	632	. . .	632	389
Intratheater airlift aircraft	458	302	760	521

Sources: William W. Kaufmann, *A Reasonable Defense* (Brookings, 1986), p. 101; and *Department of Defense Annual Report, Fiscal Year 1989*, pp. 313–15.

strategy. Concern is especially relevant because, although strategic nuclear forces get much of the attention, 85 percent of the funding goes, as it has gone for nearly thirty years, to the various components of the conventional forces.

It is hardly surprising in these circumstances that all shades of the political spectrum are calling either for actual cuts in the active-duty forces or for a greater substitution of cheaper reserves.[33] The reasons can be readily summarized: the international environment has improved, and current strategy is too conservative and should be replaced by one less demanding. Good sense as well as budget restraints and the demands of other military and nonmilitary needs therefore dictate that active-duty conventional forces be reduced commensurately and significant savings be made.

Radical reductions, however, seem unwarranted. No matter how ambitious the strategy and the Joint Chiefs' force goals associated with it, the United States, though it can maintain overseas deployments in a number of areas, has neither the ready forces nor the intercontinental mobility to reinforce more than two areas (at best) at the same time. Thus a de facto major limitation on the capabilities of the conventional forces already

33. These calls come from a variety of sources. See for example, Scowcroft and Woolsey, "Defense and Arms Control Policy," pt. 3, p. 8; and John F. Lehman, *Command of the Seas* (Scribner 1988), pp. 427–28.

exists. To cut any further, especially when the future is so uncertain, does not seem prudent, even though internationally trends in military strength appear favorable to the United States, and it is in our interest to see them continue.

Until the future becomes a little clearer, perhaps as a consequence of further arms control agreements, the better part of valor would probably be to improve the efficiency with which current capabilities are managed. Improvement means, among other things, rounding out or filling the gaps in existing ground forces and improving Army reserve units, keeping in mind that it would be impossible to train reserves to be equivalent to active-duty units without paying as much as 80 percent of active-duty costs (which is the price the Air Force has to pay for its first-class flying reserve units). Efficiency also means making better use of warning, frequently ambiguous in some respects, to prepare troops for deployment, and even to have troops pack up from time to time and randomly practice deployment.

Above all, modernization of conventional as well as nuclear forces needs to be more carefully managed. The four services still have not finished buying the current generation of weapon systems symbolized by the M-1 tank, the F-16 fighter, and the Nimitz nuclear-powered aircraft carrier. Nevertheless, they are rushing to bring a new generation of systems, such as the advanced tactical fighter and advanced technology aircraft, into service just when the United States should welcome a cease-fire in international weapons competition and when it may turn out that these systems are neither needed nor wanted. In short, as John Tower, President Bush's initial choice for secretary of defense, noted, it is time the missions of the services undergo a major review. In default of central management, excessive resources are going to some missions at the expense of others. The upshot is inadequately balanced capabilities, some of which face the turmoil of continually adapting to new weapons or to the rapid upgrading of older systems. To some of its critics, indeed, the Pentagon has become a procurement agency rather than the overall leader of the armed forces.

The Navy

The Navy is probably the worst offender where large-scale inefficiencies are concerned. It has pushed for 600 battle-force ships, which means a total of 620 or more active and reserve vessels. Its leaders have then produced a so-called maritime strategy to justify the 600-ship goal, even though the strategy is unrealistic and the forces "required" do not relate to it in any coherent way. Thus the Navy boasts of its ability to provide forward deployments in the Sea of Japan and the Norwegian Sea, to attack enemy fleets in their home ports, and to project naval firepower by means of aircraft, cruise missiles, and guns against targets on land, sea, and air. Indeed, if one were to believe all this, the Navy and the Marine Corps would be the decisive offensive factor in defeating the Soviet Union in a conventional war.

As John Lehman, former secretary of the Navy and architect of the maritime strategy, said, without maritime superiority NATO will lose.[34] But there are several inconsistencies in the Navy's inflated claims and demands. The goal of fifteen carrier battle groups (CVBGs), each costing more than $18 billion, would provide far too few carriers for the missions advocated by the Navy's leadership and too many for more plausible tasks such as attacking enemy overseas bases, providing shows of force against Libya or the like, and supporting Marine Corps assaults in the Persian Gulf or elsewhere outside the reach of land-based aircraft. Adding a brigade's worth of amphibious lift for the Marines—another nineteen expensive ships on top of the fifty-five already in the inventory—would be equally futile. It would do little to expand what the Marines can realistically be expected to do, and would certainly be irrelevant to the objectives of the maritime strategy, which envisions the corps attacking most of the Soviet perimeter, supposedly to prevent Warsaw Pact forces from seizing Western Europe.[35]

Meanwhile, as the Navy seeks to increase its power-projection capability, the vital mission of controlling key sea lanes is not being adequately funded. Several classes of destroyers and guided missile destroyers that would protect convoys are confronting block obsolescence. Only two years ago the number of deployable battle-force ships was expected to reach 605; that number is now estimated to be between 570 and 580.[36] Unfortunately, the Navy's solution to this problem—billion-dollar guided missile destroyers of the Arleigh Burke class (the DDG-51s) with their costly Aegis surveillance, tracking, and battle management systems—is unlikely to improve the situation because so few new ships can be afforded in the years ahead. Similarly, although the Los Angeles (SSN-688) class of

34. Lehman, *Command of the Seas*, p. 147.
35. *Department of Defense Annual Report, Fiscal Year 1987*, p. 183.
36. *Department of Defense Annual Report, Fiscal Year 1988*, p. 336; and *Fiscal Year 1989*, p. 314.

nuclear attack submarine is an excellent (but expensive) instrument for operating quietly in narrow waters and creating barriers to the entry of enemy ships and submarines into major shipping lanes, the Navy intends to replace at least some of them with thirty SSN-21 Seawolf submarines, which are twice as costly ($1.5 billion) and probably not much better for standard antisubmarine warfare.

These ships and submarines, along with two new aircraft carriers and more amphibious lift, are much too rich a diet for these lean times. Furthermore, increasingly expensive and sophisticated vessels mean more personnel and higher operating and support costs. To minimize these expenses yet provide the strength it needs, the Navy could easily settle for 570 active and reserve ships. It could also aim toward a less costly mix of capabilities with a greater emphasis on what is known as sea control and the protection of vital sea lanes in conjunction with the allies, whose substantial fleets the Navy tends to overlook or discount. As matters now stand, trying to cancel the two new carriers (CVN-74 and CVN-75) that Congress has already funded is probably not worthwhile. But if at least five older carriers were retired (including two, the *Midway* and the *Coral Sea*, that would be retired anyway), $2 billion per carrier battle group could be saved in operating and support expenditures in the next three years. Further investment could be saved by forgoing the costs of the service-life extension program for three of the carriers ($800 million for each). Not only would the reduction leave the Navy with twelve deployable carriers and one trainer, a number with which it operated comfortably for many of the years since World War II, but it would also release a number of surface combatants for sea-control duty and lessen the demand for expensive new escorts. On a related issue, the advanced tactical aircraft, of which the Navy plans to buy 522, is now scheduled to move into production in the early 1990s, when it will begin to replace the A-6, a medium bomber. Considering that the Navy is still buying the F/A-18 and that the future of surface combatants in general and carriers in particular is uncertain in light of improving methods of surveillance, the advanced tactical aircraft should undergo rigorous testing and evaluation during the next five years, following the example set by the Air Force with the F-117A (but with fewer aircraft). As another part of the U.S. power-projection capability, the Marine Corps can safely do without the amphibious lift for an additional brigade. And while the V-22 (Osprey) tilt-rotor aircraft ($30 billion to $35 billion for 600 planes) would be nice to have for over-the-beach operations, existing and cheaper helicopters can accomplish the same mission without any significant loss of effectiveness.

It should also be possible both to strengthen U.S. sea-control forces and to save money. Canceling the SSN-21 and continuing production of advanced versions of the SSN-688 would ensure the effectiveness of barrier operations in the western Pacific and north Atlantic. Similarly, deferring the long-range air ASW capability aircraft and further acquisition of the P-3C, along with improvements in the sound ocean surveillance system (SOSUS) and modern mines, would maintain the Navy's ability to conduct antisubmarine operations in the open ocean and over specific areas such as the Denmark Strait and the Norwegian Sea. And to add to the capability for protecting convoys, the DDG-51 could be canceled in favor of less expensive and sophisticated guided missile frigates similar to the FFG-7.

Further savings through less dependence on overseas bases, improved personnel retention, and lower operating costs could be made if the Navy would give up keeping carrier battle groups and battalion-sized Marine amphibious units on permanent station in the western Pacific and the Mediterranean.[37] A more impressive demonstration of naval power would, in any event, result from random sorties to these areas in peacetime (so that U.S. presence or absence would not be taken for granted) and appearances in force during a crisis. Indeed, such a practice would increase the probability that, in the event of a raid such as the one conducted against Libya, the Navy by itself would have the necessary decks and aircraft.

The Air Force

The Air Force has not adopted anything as exotic as the Navy's maritime strategy or as expansive as a 600-ship force—indeed, it has wisely trimmed back to 35 the goal of 44 tactical air wings envisioned at the beginning of the Reagan administration. But in an era marked by a certain lack of coordination among the services, the Air Force does want to maximize the role of its tactical air forces relative to that of the ground forces in any land combat. It also seeks to upgrade its inventory of weapon systems as rapidly as technology and resources will permit. However, precisely because of technological limitations, tactical air forces by themselves cannot prevent an enemy on the ground from advancing and seizing territory. They need enough ground forces, at a minimum, to provide a barrier against such an attack and to force the enemy both to consume

---

37. Even former Secretary of the Navy John F. Lehman, Jr., conceded that the Navy no longer has to maintain its current operating tempo. David C. Morrison, ''The Part-Time Military,'' *National Journal*, March 4, 1989, p. 520.

resources and to seek their replacement, which in turn creates strategic and tactical targets—the enemy's industrial base and its transportation network.

In the circumstances, the Air Force does not see its main function as helping to strengthen the barrier by directly supporting ground forces. Rather, it considers its principal missions as gaining air superiority over enemy tactical air forces by offensive action and then attacking the enemy's industrial base (if permitted) and crippling its transportation system. To succeed, the tactical air forces must fly deep into enemy territory, which means long-legged aircraft with complex navigation systems. Once there, they must have the munitions, accuracy, and agility to engage in air-to-air combat and to destroy airfield runways and support facilities, aircraft shelters, bridges, tunnels, railroad marshaling yards, even trains and trucks. All of which means that the Air Force must rely on a large number of specialized aircraft or a smaller number of very expensive fighter-attack aircraft. If these missions are successful and timely, the tactical air forces will have played a vital and more or less independent role in defeating the enemy. Indeed, these are precisely the objectives that the Air Force sought to attain in World War II, Korea, and Southeast Asia, with varying degrees of effectiveness. In none of these conflicts, however, can it be said that the Air Force overshadowed the Army.

Despite such results, the Air Force's doctrinal commitment to air superiority and interdiction continues. Even so, its commanders in the field assert that in a future conflict, and especially one in central Europe, if enemy units appeared to be on the verge of smashing through the allied front, the Air Force would use all available assets in direct support of the ground forces. There must remain some doubt, however, about how effective that support would be. Under pressure from then Secretary of Defense James R. Schlesinger, Jr., the Air Force reluctantly agreed to equip seven of its fighter-attack wings (five in the active-duty and two in the reserve forces) with the A-10A, an aircraft specially designed to give close air support to ground forces, but it resisted pressure from Schlesinger's successors to buy more A-10s or develop a successor aircraft.

For better or for worse, the A-10 wings constitute only 20 percent of the thirty-five fighter-attack wings that the Air Force now deploys on active duty and in the reserves. The remaining 80 percent, consisting mostly of older F-4s and the newer F-15s and F-16s along with a small number of stealth fighters (the F-117A), is designed for air superiority and interdiction and is likely to be highly vulnerable to ground fire if used for close air support. Perhaps such an allocation is inevitable, considering that there is a strong case for a quick victory in a campaign for air superiority. Still, it remains uncertain whether the subsequent interdiction effort would prove so disruptive so rapidly that it could prevent a major enemy breakthrough on the ground.

There are, of course, other missions these aircraft could perform. Perhaps the most interesting is against what has come to be called follow-on forces attacks, in which the enemy is assumed to deploy ground forces to a depth of 100 kilometers or more from the front and to attack weak points in the allied front with waves of these reserves. It is also assumed that the Army, Air Force, and our NATO allies can agree on the targets and timing of attacks and that the Air Force has the navigational aids, sensors, and munitions to disrupt or destroy the enemy follow-on forces.

These are large assumptions, and they may prove to be optimistic if the enemy changes deployments and tactics. But if combined with highly selective interdiction, attacking follow-on forces holds out more promise than an all-out interdiction campaign. Moreover, estimates suggest that U.S. and allied tactical air forces already have more than enough modern fighter-attack aircraft to win air superiority and devote a large number of sorties to a campaign against follow-on forces.[38] In the circumstances the Air Force should probably give its highest priority to improving capabilities for finding targets at night and in bad weather and to developing scatterable munitions that will have a reasonable probability of damaging armored and other tracked vehicles, which constitute the main threat to the front.

Whether the Air Force will see its nonnuclear priorities in this order is another matter. It is certainly the case that acquisition of LANTIRN (low-altitude navigation and targeting infrared system for night) and WAAM (wide-area antiarmor munitions) is proceeding. But the Air Force continues to forgo the development of new aircraft for close air support and concentrates instead on very long-range systems such as the F-15E (at $45 million a copy), the advanced tactical fighter, which will probably cost three times more ($65 billion in fiscal 1988 dollars for 500), and AMRAAM (advanced medium-range air-to-air missile) at about $500,000 a missile in the fiscal 1990 budget, despite continuing problems with identifying enemy aircraft beyond visual range in a complex battle and then obtaining a high probability of kill. Meanwhile, it now asserts that

---

38. John D. Steinbruner, "The Prospect of Cooperative Security," in Steinbruner, ed., *Restructuring American Foreign Policy,* pp. 114–16.

the F-16 can be adapted to the role of close air support as the A-16. A more prudent policy consistent with fiscal constraints, international trends, and better battlefield performance would have the Air Force proceed to develop a successor to the A-10A, as recommended by Secretary Weinberger, specifically for close air support. It should also increase production rates of the F-16 from 150 to 180 planes a year, but emphasize attacks on follow-on forces rather than close air support. It should cancel the F-15E on grounds of excessive cost and overcommitment to interdiction, and defer production of the advanced tactical fighter and AMRAAM while conducting a rigorous program of testing and evaluation for both. In short, here as elsewhere, concurrency in development and production should be ended.

The Army

Of the three services, the Army plays the most critical role in conventional warfare but gets the smallest budget both in overall terms and in the amount available for investment. For fiscal 1990 the Reagan administration requested only $80.5 billion for the Army, compared with $101.7 billion for the Navy and $100.5 billion for the Air Force. The Army will spend only 29.6 percent of its budget on investment compared with 43.5 percent by the Navy and 52 percent by the Air Force.

One reason the other services have more funding is that the Army does not contribute significantly to the strategic nuclear forces.[39] Another reason is that it appears to lack the Navy's and Air Force's fast-reaction, fire-fighting qualities so prized by presidents. A quick and exciting strike against Libya is not the Army's strength. Yet it is the Army, with 772,000 active-duty personnel and another 804,000 in the National Guard and the reserves, that must maintain vital ground forces in the forward defense of West Germany (including Berlin) and South Korea, and garrisons in other parts of the world, including Hawaii, Alaska, and Panama.[40] It must also be prepared to reinforce all these areas and have the resources to deploy as many as nine divisions to footholds in the Persian Gulf and the Caribbean. Indeed, none of the commitments to allies could be fulfilled without the presence of significant Army combat and support forces on the ground.

To produce the twenty-eight divisions deemed necessary to meet its most critical responsibilities, the Army must depend more than the other

39. *Department of Defense Annual Report, Fiscal Year 1990*, p. 220.
40. *Department of Defense Annual Report, Fiscal Year 1989*, pp. 305–06.

services on its National Guard and reserve components. From them must come the battalions and brigades necessary to bring five active-duty divisions to full combat strength. In addition, National Guard and reserve components must provide most of the support units essential to sustaining divisions in combat. And they are expected to train, mobilize, and deploy ten of the twenty-eight divisions that the Army has set as its current force goal. It is a heavy burden to place on a reserve capability that works for the most part with hand-me-down equipment and can train no more than forty days a year.

In the circumstances, one would expect the Army to continue the current wave of equipment modernization, extend it to key units in the National Guard and reserve, improve the training throughout the reserves, with more active-duty personnel involved in the process, and ensure that both active-duty and reserve forces can be deployed to trouble spots quickly. And indeed the Army is trying mightily to do just that, but it faces four serious obstacles. Since the Air Force is so penurious in providing close air support to the ground forces and since the Army is denied the right to build fixed-wing, close air support aircraft of its own, it has resorted to using expensive attack helicopters to fill what is perceived as the gap in sorties per division, although helicopters have been highly vulnerable to ground fire in Vietnam, Grenada, the Falklands, and Afghanistan. Even in Grenada, where the defenders had no sophisticated antiaircraft missiles or radar-guided guns, 30 percent of the U.S. helicopters were hit and nine were destroyed.[41]

Moreover, since the Army does not quite believe the Air Force will suppress enemy tactical air forces by quick and decisive offensive action, and since it cannot quite agree with its sister service on who should control what blocks of air space over the Army and its logistical support, it strives to create its own air defense umbrella with both low- and high-altitude surface-to-air missiles (SAMs).

As if AH-64 attack helicopters and Patriot SAMs were not enough of a diversion of resources from the ground forces, the Army has come to suffer from the same desire to accelerate the rollover of its inventory of platforms that has afflicted the other services. It is now striving to acquire what amount to new tanks, new air defenses, new helicopters, new antitank weapons (that can also serve as air defense weapons), and new missiles to go after enemy follow-on forces even though it has not yet completed

41. Lehman, *Command of the Seas*, p. 303.

the current wave of modernization and will not have the resources to do both.

Finally, since the Army does not control the airlift and sealift that would deliver its forces to overseas theaters and has little direct leverage with the Navy and Air Force to provide these services adequately, it has more forces than can be readily deployed and sustained. Even worse, it lacks the incentive to make its equipment easily transportable by air, although General John A. Wickham, Jr., while Army chief of staff, attempted a partial solution to the problem with the creation of light divisions, which now appear to have fallen into disfavor precisely because of their lack of heavy armor and firepower.

Without a bold intervention from the secretary of defense, the Army cannot do much on its own to resolve the close air support and air defense issues. It simply lacks the resources to go beyond what it is already doing to supplement or duplicate the performance of these missions by the Air Force. What it can do, however, is continue modernization with the current generation of weapon systems and resist the temptation to rush into the deployment of the next generation before it is fully tested and evaluated. In other words, even within the constraint of a nominal freeze, the Army will have the resources to buy more advanced M-1 Abrams tanks at $3 million each, M-2 Bradley fighting vehicles at $1 million each (or a lot more upgraded M-113 armored personnel carriers that do not pretend to be tanks), AH-64 Apache attack helicopters ($13 million each), Patriot SAM batteries ($1 million a missile), Stinger and TOW missiles, self-propelled artillery, and trucks. However, if it proceeds in that direction, as it almost certainly should, it will have to defer production on such next-generation systems as LHX (light helicopter, experimental) at $35 billion to $40 billion for some 2,100; FAADS (forward-area air defense system); ATACMS (army tactical missile system); and JSTAR (joint surveillance–target attack radar system). Restraint, which would be dictated primarily by scarce resources and caution about the relative efficiency of the next generation of systems, might also be interpreted as a response to Mikhail Gorbachev's intention to reduce his own ground forces in the next two years. The Army should make a virtue of necessity.

Strategic Mobility

A strategy of forward defense carries with it the implication that the United States and its allies will not trade space for the time in which to mobilize and deploy additional forces. Consequently, intercontinental or strategic mobility and the timely movement of reinforcements is essential. Although nearly 25 percent of U.S. active-duty personnel are stationed overseas on land or afloat, the bulk of the U.S. conventional capability (active and reserve) remains in the continental United States and would have to be transported to key theaters abroad in the event of a crisis. Indeed, it is often forgotten that if a serious confrontation occurred between the United States and the Soviet Union, all U.S. theater commanders would understandably begin clamoring for their share of available reinforcements, given the inevitable uncertainty as to whether a specific conventional conflict, especially in Europe, could be contained.

In principle, there are five ways to respond to these demands. Instead of stationing some forces overseas and holding most reinforcements in the United States, the Defense Department could change the ratio and place more troops in key theaters such as Western Europe and Northeast Asia. The political and budgetary costs of such a change would far outweigh any potential benefits, however, and it is not considered a serious option. An alternative is to pre-position heavy equipment and supplies in selected theaters and fly in units to marry with them. Although this costs up to $5 billion for a full division's worth of equipment, the United States currently has four full sets in West Germany and plans to increase that number to six. In any event, the cost is not as great as it sounds, since other units, presumably from the reserves, would inherit the equipment left behind by the forces deploying abroad. A variant of land-based pre-positioning is to load specialized ships with equipment and supplies and station them in the vicinity of trouble spots. During a crisis the ships would steam to a friendly port or even a beach to await the arrival of troops flown in to take over the materiel. At present the United States deploys twelve such ships in the Indian Ocean and several others in the Atlantic and in Far Eastern waters.[42] Still another way to respond is to maintain a fleet of aircraft with sufficient capacity to move both personnel and equipment to overseas destinations. This option, along with pre-positioning, has found the greatest favor in the Defense Department for many years and has been the basis for acquiring a fleet of C-5, C-141, and KC-10A aircraft as well as modifying a number of wide-bodied commercial aircraft in the civil reserve air fleet to carry military cargoes in an emergency.[43] Finally, it is possible by means of fast sealift to move

42. *Department of Defense Annual Report, Fiscal Year 1988*, pp. 228–30; *Fiscal Year 1989*, pp. 219–23; and *Fiscal Year 1990*, p. 173.
43. *Department of Defense Annual Report, Fiscal Year 1989*, p. 315.

large cargoes from U.S. seaports to overseas theaters in a relatively few days. The United States now has eight such ships (SL-7s) and a number of tanker and cargo ships under government control, with a total capacity that will reach 895,000 short tons in the early 1990s.[44]

The current mixture of land and sea pre-positioning, airlift, and sealift should permit the simultaneous delivery of the equivalent of ten divisions to Europe and another three or four to the Persian Gulf during the first thirty days of a U.S. mobilization and deployment. South Korea could also be reinforced by the Marine division in Okinawa or the Army infantry division in Hawaii. Thus in principle the existing system has sufficient capacity to meet the demands of any plausible U.S. strategy. However, there are doubts about its ability to do so in practice. The possibility always exists that an enemy would try to interfere with the process, although the diversity of the system gives some insurance against such an eventuality. Perhaps more important is whether the system is sufficiently well organized and rehearsed to ensure that such a large deployment could take place in so short a time. Most troubling of all is that the United States might not have a grace period as long as thirty days because of enemy attacks after only a brief period of warning, because American decision-makers would fritter away much of the warning time before putting the systems into operation, or because the warning would be too ambiguous to warrant mobilization. To guard against these last dangers, planners in the Defense Department have tended to stress pre-positioning and airlift to the detriment of fast sealift. The Air Force, in particular, claims a mandate to expand its airlift capacity to 66 million ton-miles a day from the current level of about 46 million and proposes to acquire 211 C-17A airlift aircraft at a cost of more than $35 billion in fiscal 1988 dollars to reach its goal.[45] However, such an investment may not be worth its cost when it would add only 4,500 tons delivered to Europe each day, or 135,000 tons a month. In two weeks fast sealift could deliver the same amount of tonnage for about 5 percent of the cost of the C-17A. Thus sealift appears the better buy.

To resupply U.S. forces in a large-scale conflict could take between 7 million and 10 million tons a month. The United States and its allies have

44. *Budget of the United States Government, Fiscal Year 1990*, p. 5-10.

45. *Budget of the United States Government, Fiscal Year 1990*, p. 5-10; *Department of Defense Annual Report, Fiscal Year 1989*, p. 220; *Fiscal Year 1990*, p. 173; and Kaufmann, "Defense Agenda," p. 62.

the shipping capacity to meet these and other demands, but they may not be organized adequately for such a large effort. And while the allies have enough surface combatants to escort their own convoys, it is doubtful that the U.S. Navy (given its heavy emphasis on power projection in recent years) could supply the ninety or more helicopter-equipped escorts needed to protect its shipping (assuming ten escorts for each convoy). Although the Navy might argue that attacking enemy fleets in their home ports would minimize the danger to convoys, such attacks would probably not significantly reduce the threat from submarines. That is why it makes sense to switch surface combatants out of the carrier force and buy more frigates.

Budget Comparisons

Even a modest review of current defense programs shows that savings can be achieved without weakening U.S. military capabilities. In fact, taking resources from some of the more ambitious programs and applying them to less exciting but more essential needs such as escort and mine warfare ships and fast sealift could strengthen those capabilities. But can enough be saved to permit the Defense Department to fulfill its current responsibilities and live within the budget that Congress is likely to impose? Or will the necessary savings result in a hollowing-out of the force?

Much depends on where Congress and the administration come out on defense budget authority and outlays and on specific allocations of budget authority. But suppose what currently appears to be the worst case—that Congress finally settles on a nominal freeze in Defense Department budget authority, which means that, using optimistic department inflation estimates, real budget authority will decline by an average 3 percent a year. Such a decision applied over the next five years would mean that about $230 billion in current dollars would have to be cut out of the Carlucci five-year program (not counting the reductions already assumed but not specified) and, depending on where the cuts were made, that savings in outlays could amount to about $200 billion (table 20).

If the bulk of these cuts were made in the investment accounts and other accounts were adjusted accordingly, a nominal freeze would differ from the Carlucci five-year plan for fiscal 1990–94 by the amounts shown in table 21. The appropriations for military personnel would remain the same. Funds for operation and maintenance and military family housing in the nominal freeze would total $24.2 billion less than those proposed

Table 20. Carlucci Five-Year Defense Plan and a Nominal Freeze, Budget Authority and Outlays, Fiscal Years 1990–94
Billions of current dollars

Item	1990	1991	1992	1993	1994	Total
Authority						
Carlucci plan	305.6	320.9	335.7	350.7	365.6	1,678.5
Nominal freeze	290.2	290.2	290.2	290.2	290.2	1,451.0
Difference	15.4	30.7	45.5	60.5	75.4	227.5
Outlays						
Carlucci plan	293.8	304.7	316.3	329.4	343.5	1,587.7
Nominal freeze	278.6	278.6	278.6	278.6	278.6	1,393.0
Difference	15.2	26.1	37.7	50.8	64.9	194.7

Sources: *Budget of the United States Government, Fiscal Year 1990, Historical Tables*, tables 3-3, 5-1; and author estimates.

by Carlucci. However, the difference could be more than covered either by the receipt of offsets from Japan and West Germany to pay for maintenance and improvement of U.S. military facilities in the two countries and for the U.S. hiring of their civilians or by somewhat deeper cuts in the investment accounts. Military construction would also go down by $9.9 billion in the nominal freeze because of base closings and because new construction would not be needed to accommodate such questionable systems as the B-2, the small ICBM, the rail garrison MX, and the advanced tactical fighter. Nor would construction be needed to provide for the dispersal of the fleet to additional bases (strategic home porting), a proposal that on military grounds never made sense in the first place.

Table 21. Cumulative Costs of Carlucci Five-Year Defense Plan and a Nominal Freeze, by Appropriation Title, Fiscal Years 1990–94
Billions of current dollars

Title	Carlucci plan	Nominal freeze	Saving
Military personnel	421.9	421.9	. . .
Operation and maintenance	492.5	474.0	18.5
Procurement	496.5	340.7	155.8
Research, development, test, and evaluation	211.5	177.3	34.2
Military construction	32.4	22.5	9.9
Family housing	19.7	14.0	5.7
Other[a]	4.3	0.7	3.6
Total	1,678.8	1,451.1	227.7

Sources: *Budget of the United States Government, Fiscal Year 1990, Historical Tables*, table 5-1; and author estimates.

a. Special foreign currency program, revolving and management funds, and trust funds, receipts, and accruals.

More than 80 percent of the net reductions would come from procurement and research, development, testing, and evaluation. These accounts would be reduced by $209 billion, or more than necessary, to make room for procurement and RDT&E not currently in the Carlucci plan (table 22). The strategic nuclear forces program would be reduced by more than $113 billion, largely because of deferred production of the B-2 bomber, cancelation of the rail garrison MX, and reductions in procurement of the D-5 missile and development of the strategic defense initiative. Programs for the conventional forces would lose $95.4 billion with the deferral of such systems as LHX, FAADS, ATF, and AMRAAM and cancelation of others, including the DDG-51, several amphibious ships, and the V-22 aircraft. New programs, which would include development of a smaller ballistic missile submarine and follow-on aircraft for close air support, as well as the acquisition of frigates, fast sealift ships, and heavy airlift aircraft (C5-B), would cost just over $18 billion. As a consequence, the net available reduction of $190.9 billion is slightly higher than the required goal of $189.9 billion. The remaining $1 billion could be allocated to improving the military capability of the reserves.

Force Comparisons

Since the nominal freeze is reached primarily by deferring next-generation weapons for the coming five years and removing some of the duplication and impracticality from the strategic nuclear programs, the size and composition of the forces it supports do not differ greatly from the military posture that the Carlucci defense plan would maintain. The strategic nuclear forces may have slightly fewer launchers and warheads, but they will have at least as much retaliatory power. Under the proposed allocation the Army will continue to field twenty-eight active-duty and reserve divisions, the Marines will retain their four divisions and air wings (three active and one reserve), and the Air Force will operate at least thirty-five active and reserve fighter-attack wings. The Navy will be slightly smaller and its composition somewhat changed, but it will still be able to perform essential power-projection missions and sea-control forces will increase in size and effectiveness.[46] Strategic mobility will benefit from

---

46. *Department of Defense Annual Report, Fiscal Year 1989*, pp. 314–15; and *Budget of the United States Government, Fiscal Year 1989*, pp. 5-8–5-9.

Table 22.   Investment Savings from a Nominal Freeze, by Program,
Fiscal Years 1990–94
Billions of current dollars

	Estimated Carlucci plan		Nominal freeze		
Programs	*Procurement*	*RDT&E*[a]	*Procurement*	*RDT&E*[a]	*Saving*
Existing programs					
Strategic nuclear forces	116.4	65.5	34.4	33.9	113.6
Tactical nuclear forces	2.4	. . .	2.4	. . .	. . .
Conventional forces					
Tracked vehicles	24.4	8.9	24.4	8.9	. . .
Helicopters	23.0	6.9	23.0	6.9	. . .
Army air defense system	8.9	2.7	0.8	2.7	8.1
Air Force combat aircraft	38.8	29.1	30.6	27.0	11.3
Navy and USMC aircraft	51.8	33.1	37.5	28.6	18.8
Service and support aircraft	20.1	4.0	9.6	4.0	10.5
Major warships and submarines	53.5	10.7	24.1	10.7	29.4
Other ships	12.3	2.5	12.3	2.5	. . .
Ship conversions	5.9	. . .	5.9	. . .	. . .
Airlift aircraft	9.3	8.9	2.0	8.9	7.3
Tactical missiles and torpedoes	33.8	6.8	33.8	6.8	. . .
NATO initiatives	2.8	0.6	2.8	0.6	. . .
Intelligence and communications	28.8	19.0	23.8	19.0	5.0
Classified programs	64.2	12.8	59.2	12.8	5.0
Total existing programs	496.4	211.5	326.6	173.3	209.0
New programs					
Development of smaller ballistic missile submarines	. . .	. . .	. . .	2.0	−2.0
NATO barrier (one-third of total cost)	. . .	. . .	0.9	. . .	−0.9
Development of new close-air-support attack aircraft	. . .	. . .	. . .	2.0	−2.0
16 FFG-X (new guided missile frigates)	. . .	. . .	6.4	. . .	−6.4
21 C-5B heavy airlift aircraft	. . .	. . .	2.0	. . .	−2.0
2 maritime pre-positioning ships	. . .	. . .	0.8	. . .	−0.8
20 fast sealift ships	. . .	. . .	4.0	. . .	−4.0
Total new programs	. . .	. . .	14.1	4.0	−18.1
Total	496.4	211.5	340.7	177.3	190.9

Sources: Kaufmann, "Defense Agenda," pp. 90–92; and author estimates.
a. Research, development, test, and evaluation.

Table 23. Procurement under a Nominal Freeze, by Program, Fiscal Years 1990–94

Program	Number	Funding (*billions of current dollars*)
Strategic nuclear forces		
Advanced cruise missile	840	5.1
Trident II submarine	5	8.1
Trident II (D-5) ballistic missile	168	6.1
KC-135 re-engining	250	4.5
Other procurement	. . .	21.4
Tactical nuclear forces		
Tomahawk land-attack missile, nuclear (TLAM-N)	308	2.4
Other procurement	. . .	1.8
Conventional forces		
Tanks	5,000	11.0
Other tracked vehicles	7,000	12.2
Helicopters	1,700	12.9
Combat aircraft	2,000	46.8
Service and support aircraft	866	9.6
Major warships	31	21.3
Other warships and auxiliaries	72	5.9
Airlift aircraft	21	2.0
Sealift and maritime pre-positioning ships	22	4.8
Tactical missiles and torpedoes	180,000	22.0
Other procurement	. . .	103.3
Intelligence and communications		
Satellite equivalents	66	22.9
Other procurement	. . .	16.6
Total	. . .	340.7

Sources: Author estimates based on Kaufmann, "Defense Agenda," pp. 78–79, 90–91.

a somewhat larger heavy airlift capacity and a greatly expanded fast sealift. Moreover, a substantial program of modernization can still be afforded within the constraints of a nominal freeze (table 23). Advanced cruise missiles, five more Trident submarines, a significant number of D-5 missiles, and improved surveillance, early warning, navigational, and communications capabilities could be added to the nuclear forces. The conventional forces could be equipped with 5,000 new M-1 tanks and 7,000 other tracked vehicles, 1,700 more helicopters, an additional 2,000 combat aircraft, 31 more major warships, and 180,000 modern torpedoes and tactical missiles. In short, $340.7 billion over five years can still buy a lot of military capability, even though the total funding available for procurement has been cut by nearly $156 billion from its projected level (table 22). Moreover, given the tremendous amounts of hardware that the Reagan buildup purchased during the 1980s, the United States will have a first-rate force for the rest of this century.

In the same vein, more than $177 billion for research, development, testing, and evaluation can also accomplish a great deal. Few major weapon systems would be canceled, but equally few of the next-generation capabilities would be moved from research, development, testing, and evaluation into production. What many may see as a case of arrested development would not, however, occur simply because of budgetary constraints or a Luddite opposition to new technology. In light of the difficulties the Defense Department has encountered when bringing new weapons into the inventory, it has become essential to have an active research and development program to hedge against the uncertainties of the future and to ensure that systems really work as intended before they go into production. And considering developments on the international scene, it hardly makes sense to rush into a very expensive modernization program when the prospects for arms control are at least interesting, and efforts to change the military status quo, however well intentioned, could be misunderstood. Should events turn out propitiously, money will have been saved; should the Soviet Union turn sour again, the United States will be in a strong position to upgrade its forces rapidly and protect its interests.

Congress, of course, may prefer to see the next generation of weapons go forward to production and instead achieve the necessary savings by cuts in minor procurement and operation and maintenance. However, because the requisite amounts are so large, it would be difficult to take them out of these accounts without inflicting deep and obvious wounds on the national defense. More balanced forces, a five-year perspective, and a somewhat slower rate at which savings in outlays are made may not be the perfect prescription for the foreseeable future. But it is to be hoped that, as a seventeenth-century bishop commented when he threw a stone at a dog and hit his mother-in-law, even if the intention is imperfectly fulfilled, the effort is not entirely wasted.

Conclusion

Since the United States somewhat reluctantly assumed the burdens of a world power after World War II, it has never spent sufficient funds on defense to carry out simultaneously all its declared commitments and various military strategies. The funds made available to defense in the past forty-five years have resulted from a combination of factors: the magnitude of the perceived threat, the international environment, and the internal political and economic situation. For better or worse, this nation has now achieved a bipartisan consensus on the approximate level of resources that will be made available to defense in the first part of the 1990s. The challenge for the Bush administration and Congress is to apply those resources in a way that relates them to a coherent strategy and the changing international environment. Nothing will be gained from complaining about the level of resources or allowing the military services to share the resources in accordance with their priorities. In a world of cold war and worst-case scenarios it may not be possible to devise a defense plan that honors both coherence and current fiscal constraints. However, such a plan remains feasible in the world now faced by the United States. Indeed, under a new administration, a strong and enlightened leadership has a real opportunity to put the elements of a reasonable program into place despite the relative scarcity of resources. By contrast, a leadership dedicated to laissez-faire will give the nation the worst of all possible worlds: a widening gap between strategy and resources and a force structure inappropriate to the current international environment.